T0068139

FROM
DIVORCE
TO
DEBTORS'
PRISON

A Court That Uses
"The Best Interest of the Child"
To Bring Back Debtors' Prison

Delilah Daney

WESTBOW
PRESS®
A DIVISION OF THOMAS NELSON
& ZONDERVAN

WestBow Press books may be ordered through booksellers or by contacting:

WestBow Press
A Division of Thomas Nelson & Zondervan
1663 Liberty Drive
Bloomington, IN 47403
www.westbowpress.com
844-714-3454

Scripture taken from the King James Version of the Bible.

ISBN: 978-1-6642-5318-6 (sc)
ISBN: 978-1-6642-5319-3 (hc)
ISBN: 978-1-6642-5320-9 (e)

Library of Congress Control Number: 2022901741

Print information available on the last page.

WestBow Press rev. date: 02/21/2022

DEDICATION

I want to thank God and give Him all the glory for giving me the strength and courage to speak up for what I see as something that is wrong and for being with all of us even in circumstances that we don't understand. We serve a great God, who walks with us on this journey called life.

I want to dedicate this book to my husband, my best friend, who was there to encourage me and support me in my writing. To all the people who have been hurt by laws that hurt families and not help them.

To my parents for teaching me about God.

I pray for all the fathers that want to do what's right for their children and that God will hear their prayers. God created the family not our government.

FOREWORD

In Matthew 7: 1-2, 12 KJV

Judge not, that ye will not be judged. For with what judgment ye judge, ye shall be judged: and with what measure ye mete, it shall be measured to you again.

Therefore, all things whatsoever ye would that men should do to you, do ye even so to them, for this is the Law and the Prophets.

God gave us Ten Commandments to follow-

The first four are about our relationship with God and the last six are about our relationship with one another.

God told us to love Him and to love one another. Lawmakers did not create family; therefore, it is not their place to judge it when it gets broken, especially with such treachery as this.

I am writing this to help me and hopefully others to understand what our legal system is doing to the family unit when it gets broken. The laws that are made do not work in every situation and cause more stress to a stressful situation.

This is a true story, but names have been changed to protect the people involved.

CONTENTS

CONTENTS

Marriage/ Divorce
What does God say?

In Mathew 19: 4-6 KJV

And He answered and said to them, "Have ye not read, that He which made them at the beginning made them male and female and said "For this cause shall a man leave father and mother and shall cleave to his wife: and they twain shall be one flesh. Wherefore they are no more twain but one flesh. What therefore God hath joined together, let not man put asunder.

God created man first and then woman from man. They were created to, as it is said in Genesis 1: 28 KJV... To be fruitful and multiply; and replenish the earth and subdue it.

God created marriage to be as the wedding vows state: till death do us part. When a man and a woman love God and put Him first in their marriage, it is such a gift and a blessing. The marriage covenant was created by God to protect not only the man and the woman but also the children.

In Malachi 2: 14,15 KJV. Yet ye say, wherefore? Because the Lord hath been witness between thee and the wife of thy youth, against whom thou hast dealt treacherously; yet is she thy companion, and the wife of thy covenant. And did not he make one? Yet had he the residue of the spirit. And wherefore one? That he might seek a godly seed. Therefore, take heed to your spirit, and let none deal treacherously against the wife of his youth.

There are so many scriptures that refer to marriage and that it is a covenant between God and a man and a woman.

This is a basic marriage covenant:

I.....take .... to be my wife (or husband). To have and to hold from this day forward, for better, for worse, for richer, for poorer, in sickness and health, to love and cherish, till death do us part, according to God's holy law; and this is my solemn vow.

In Matthew 19: 8 & 9 KJV When Jesus was asked why the law permitted divorce. He saith unto them, Moses because of the hardness of your hearts suffered you to put away your wives; but from the beginning it was not so. And I say unto you, whosoever shall put away his wife, except it be for fornication, and shall marry another committeth adultery; and whoso marrieth her which is put away doth commit adultery.

God knows everything about us. He sees our hearts and He knows what we think, say and do. We should not enter a covenant lightly that is so important to our loving God. There are spouses who try to harm the other spouse. I was told by a man that his wife tried poisoning him and a woman who was physically, emotionally and psychologically abused by her husband. When the abused spouse turns to God for help because they do not want to break the covenant they made and yet they know in their hearts that the person they are married to might eventually kill them. I know God sees and knowing both of their hearts. Even though, God hates divorce; He knows the pain that is caused by breaking what He created for our good. To God a covenant is an unbreakable commitment.

Unfortunately, when we marry a spouse who is not someone who truly loves God, they are not going to understand the seriousness of the covenant they are making. That doesn't excuse their actions and that they violated a vow or covenant that they made before God. We will all be accountable for the mistakes we make, but thanks be to God for sending His son Jesus and giving us all second chances. 2 Corinthians 6:14 KJV "Be ye not unequally yoked together with unbelievers for what fellowship hath righteousness with unrighteousness? And what communion hath light with darkness? I have also heard the term unequally matched.

This was written in a book called "Unequally Yoked Wives" by Dr. C.S. Lovett. This was found on a crinkled piece of paper that Alice found. The following is quoted in the book.

"If your marriage is producing un-Christ like thoughts and feelings in you, it could be dangerous. It is possible to receive spiritual injury within a marriage from which a Christian may never recover. And the real tragedy of it is one is forced to enter heaven's marriage in that damaged condition. Watch, therefore. Look closely to see what your earthly marriage is doing to you. Is it preparing you to live with Jesus or is it disqualifying you? How can it disqualify you? By turning you into a hostile, bitter person. You can pray all you like, but if living with an unsaved man under pearl/swine conditions is making you unlike Jesus, you are slowly being destroyed by something God intended for your good. When a temporary earthly marriage situation begins to produce eternal damage in a child of God, it is time to run. Don't walk, run."

CHAPTER 2

From deception in marriage to divorce
Alice and Frank's Story

The people I will be referring to in this book will be Alice an abused woman who was married to Aaron, and Frank who was married to a woman referred to as Jezebel.

Alice was taught that a marriage was something that needed to be worked on. When she realized, she was married to a man that didn't truly love her and didn't want to work with her to make it work. She was too ashamed to share with anyone how he was treating her. She always remembered a saying," You made your bed now you have to lie in it". She felt trapped and hopeless and didn't know what to do. She tried counseling with a priest when they were living on the west coast, not talking about the abuse, the priest told her to go home and be a good wife and mother. Alice tried her best, but when she realized she was with the wrong person because he made her feel that she didn't have any worth or value. The only thing she knew to do was to pray and try to find an answer in God's word. When her husband got a job on the east coast, she had to follow him in a car. He would not tell her what route they were taking and would drive faster than the speed limit until he would be out of her sight. She would keep driving on the road and hoped she would find him (she didn't have a map or GPS or a cell phone). Occasionally he would slow down when he didn't see her. It was a nightmare following him in a car, as much as it was living with him. When they finally got to where they were moving to on the east coast. They rented a condo for a short time until they found a house. When they were going to move into the house it needed carpet, so when Alice had something to take care of, Aaron and a woman at the carpet store picked out the carpet for the house. Alice suspected that something was going on but didn't know what to do about it. One time a woman called the house asking for her husband and when Alice asked who was calling, the woman asked if she was his mother. When Alice said no, I'm his wife, the woman hung up.

Alice started going to a church and the priest could tell there was something wrong. He started counseling her and praying with her. Telling her how precious she was to Jesus. Alice asked Jesus to come into her life and realized she had value and worth and shouldn't be treated the way Aaron was treating her.

The first time Alice left her husband, Aaron, she put whatever she could into the car, and told her children to only bring their favorite things with them. They had to limit what they brought. She believed they were not coming back. They drove from where they were living in the southeast to the northeast without letting her husband know. She left around 2pm and drove all night (she had never driven for that distance alone). Alice and the children arrived in the state below their destination around 6am and called her mom from a pay phone to get directions to her place (Alice didn't have a map or GPS or a cell phone). Her Mom had moved after the death of her dad to be closer to her sister. Alice's husband had called her mom in the morning after she had called her. (Alice had asked her husband if she could follow some other women who were heading up north early that week so she could visit her mom and he told her she couldn't. So that's why he knew to call her mom when he couldn't figure out where she was). Before Alice had gotten to her mom's place, Aaron was taking a plane up to her mom's place. When he had arrived, he had his gun and his golf clubs with him. Alice's Mom had concerns about what was going on, but she felt that they had to work it out. Her Mom took a long walk with Aaron and believed him when he told her that he really loved Alice. Alice didn't want to go back, but she felt as though she didn't have any choice. Her Mom was living in a condo for people fifty and over, she knew she couldn't stay with her, and she didn't have a job, so she went back with Aaron.

In 1 Corinthians 7: 13KJV And the woman which hath an husband that believeth not, and if he be pleased to dwell with her, let her not leave him.

The next time Alice left was because Aaron started arguing with her about something, the next thing she knew he had ripped the night gown she was wearing down the front, and then threw her toward the couch. When she hit the couch, (which was a sofa bed with a metal frame) she hurt the side of her right knee and ankle. The next day she went to church and the priest knew there was something wrong especially since she was limping a bit. On Monday, she went to talk to the priest. He took pictures of the bruises on her leg and arm. This is when he recommended that she go to a woman's shelter. While Alice was at the woman's shelter, she met a woman who had told her that her husband had slammed her against a wall while she was pregnant with one of her children. It reminded Alice of the time she thought she was pregnant and told her husband and he told her if she were pregnant, he would make her get an abortion. It helped Alice to understand that it wasn't her but that there were other women being abused by their spouses or boyfriends. Alice and her children spent a week at the shelter and after going to court to have Aaron move out of the house she returned to the house. When she was supposed to return to the house, she asked for the police to assist with her return because she was afraid of what her husband might do. The police came, but back then the laws didn't take violence in the home as serious. She felt like the two police officers thought her fears were not to be taken seriously.

Her husband had convinced some people from the church that he wanted to get back with Alice. The people from the church told Alice that her husband had accepted Jesus as his Lord and Savior. Alice wanted to believe this was true because she knew that would be the only way that their marriage could be healed. So again, Alice let Aaron move back in. She remembers seeing the look on the priest's face when they walked into church together. The priest didn't believe Aaron had changed and was annoyed that the people in the church had interfered in something that they really didn't understand. It wasn't long before Aaron started acting like his old self. Alice remembers on New Year's Eve how Aaron had said that there was going to be a party on base that he wanted to go to. He had told Alice and the children that he would go to the roller-skating rink with them that night. It was open until 1am that night. Aaron dropped them off and didn't return until closing.

The next day while Alice and Aaron were in the kitchen. Aaron started criticizing and speaking to Alice in a demeaning manner. She felt she couldn't take it anymore. She had a towel in her hand as she was taking dishes out of the dishwasher. She rolled it to try to snap it at his butt (she never could do it before) but suddenly it worked, and she got him right on the butt. He turned around and grabbed her and smashed her face into the handle on one of the cabinets. She didn't feel like she had hurt him and yet he came at her with such hate and anger. What had changed at that moment was this: before when he would hurt her, he would apologize and try to pretend he was sorry. Then afterwards he would act like nothing had happened. This time he acted like she deserved what he did to her and wasn't sorry he did it.

Alice kept praying to God, asking to help her and her marriage. After about a few months suddenly Aaron decided, he was going to move out. 1 Corinthians 7: 15 KJV But if the unbeliever depart, let him depart: but God hath called us to peace. Aaron had been gone a week and the children didn't even know that he had moved out.

Even though, Aaron had moved out, he would sneak into the house in the middle of the night when everyone was sound asleep and rape Alice. She was afraid he would hurt the children, so she never said anything. He would do his thing and leave. Alice never told anyone, she kept praying to God and asking Him to make him stop. The priest that she used to counsel with had moved and she didn't have anyone to talk with about what was happening.

When Aaron was ready to get a divorce, he brought Alice to an attorney that was so bitter from his own divorce that Alice had to leave the office. Alice was able to get an attorney recommended to her from the shelter where she had stayed. Even though, her husband had abandoned them, Alice's attorney advised her to settle for whatever she could get and get away from him (because of the abuse). They had filed for separation on May 29, and it seemed, as though, God had opened doors, they were divorced exactly 30 days after. This was the exact number of days required by the state they were living in. Originally the divorce date was scheduled for July 3, but the attorney found out the court was going to be closed that day. The attorney was able to get the divorce settlement squeezed in on June 30. Alice felt that God was releasing her of the vows she had taken because God knew Aaron's heart. She knew her children and she needed to start the healing process, which she knew was going to be a long and painful process.

She knew God would be with her as He always has been. That doesn't mean it was going to be easy.

Alice's mom had come to stay with them and was there to help her with the move. Her brother-in-law and nephews flew down to help also. On the long drive, the children's hamsters died, one of their cats got scared and when they opened the car door it took off into the woods and they couldn't find it. They drove for two days and ran into a bad rainstorm where you could hardly see the car in front of you. Eventually they got to their destination safely. Alice knew God's hand had been with them even with the few bumps they ran into.

Alice tried finding a job, but after not working outside the home for ten years. It was hard for her to find a job that could support them. She went to college for one year for Medical Records but found out that she wouldn't be making enough. Someone suggested she try Dental Hygiene. The course was difficult, and she had to find people to work on. She was new in the area and didn't know many people and searching through medical records was something she didn't have time for. As soon as she was done with classes, she had to hurry home to take care of the children.

Alice's mom was in her late sixties when they moved up. Her mom could not handle the struggles the children were going through. Alice completed as much of the Dental Hygiene course as she could, but after finishing two semesters, she was told that her clinical grade was not high enough and would have to repeat the second semester. Alice was too stressed with trying to be everything to the children and trying to get an education. Something had to go, and she loved her children too much not to take care of their needs. She trusted that God would provide.

Alice recalls her ex-husband coming to visit the children the year after they were divorced. He came up on a weekend and asked Alice if she would change her mind and consider remarrying him. She told him no. She found out shortly after that he had gotten married to someone else the day before both of their children's birthday, approximately a week after his visit with them. What was his purpose of asking Alice to marry him when he had plans to marry someone else a week later? What kind of a mind game was that? What if Alice had said yes? Then would he have laughed in her face and told her too bad I found someone else. Alice remembered a woman telling her a story about how her abusive husband did that very thing to her. She left her husband when she found out he was with another woman. He told her he didn't want her or their son or the unborn child she was carrying. She moved to the west coast back in her hometown and met someone she knew when she was growing up. He helped her when her second son was born as well as her mom and she felt like her life was doing so much better, then suddenly her husband shows up and says he wants her and the children back. She believed him and went back with him. When she got back to their home, she found out he was still with the other woman. She told me she had a nervous breakdown, fortunately her mother-in-law helped her, and she was able to be strong enough to leave him again and get divorced. She came back to the west coast and started over again. Alice felt that woman's story was something that she needed to hear especially when Aaron basically tried to pull the same thing on her.

Alice found a job that was across the street from the apartment where they were living. It was a minimum wage job, but she could walk and be there for the children.

Thank God Alice's mom was able to help her financially so that Alice could be there for the children.

Alice's son wanted a dad, but God knew Alice wasn't ready. So many people are so quick to jump into new relationships when they still haven't been healed of the relationship they just got out of. Alice struggled being a single mom. She had been praying for a Christian man to come into her life, someone who would love her and her children. A year after they were there, she met a Christian guy, but she felt he was just interested in her and not the children. So, she broke off that relationship after three months. She kept praying for the right man to come into her life and she knew she would have to wait.

Many people don't' want their children to do without the material things, but children need the love and correction of God-fearing parents. Whether it is one or two parents in the home, children need to learn about God, and how good He is. God's word says He will provide and learning to trust Him is something we all need to do.

It's amazing how little financially you can get by when there is faith and love in a home. She is not saying it is easy because it isn't. She couldn't give her children the things that most children get with two parents. She was thankful that she could have a place to live, food to eat, clothes and shoes to wear. When you get divorced, you get out of one situation but there are other situations you must handle. Doing it with God's help makes it better not easier.

Alice learned years later that how a man treats his wife is how the children treat the mother. Now Alice understands why her children gave her such a hard time and made life more difficult than it should have been. They were just copying what they saw their father do to their mother. It affects their lives and the spouses they end up choosing to spend their lives with.

11

Alice was thankful to have two parents who brought her to church and taught her about God. She just regrets that it took her a lifetime of mistakes to understand the being equally yoked thing.

So many people don't realize how important it is for the wife and husband/ father to be a man who follows God. There wouldn't be so many divorces if we could understand the importance of marrying someone who loves Jesus more than anything.

Alice met Frank when he moved to the same apartment buildings where she had been living for seven years.

This is Frank's story

Frank grew up in the small town, he had met his first wife whom I am going to refer to as Jezebel (Jezebel in the bible was known as a scheming, wicked woman). He had met her at the church he had been attending all his life. When he met her, she led him to believe that she was a church going person and believed in the same things that Frank believed in. Jezebel wasn't a stable person and Frank eventually found out but unfortunately for him he found out too late. Frank felt compassion for her and thought he could help her by showing her what real love was. Their relationship was one of her controlling the relationship from the beginning. Frank could only call her at certain times because she was living at home with her parents. They had an on again off again relationship that ended after a year. One day they ran into one another and decided to start dating again. Frank felt things had changed and seemed a little more normal when they had gotten back together the second time. After dating for a while, Frank proposed and gave Jezebel a very expensive diamond. Jezebel didn't like it and told him she wanted a more expensive ring. Frank wanted to please her and didn't think anything of it. At one point, one of Frank's sisters had warned him not to marry her because she had found out what kind of person Jezebel really was. Jezebel's parents had shared with her that they couldn't control Jezebel when she was younger, so instead of working with her, they sent her off to a boarding school. Frank was sure he could work things out with her, but as he would find out, he was wrong.

On the day of their wedding, Frank couldn't find Jezebel for three hours during the reception. When he finally found her, she was upstairs in a room with her parents. He didn't understand what was going on and apparently no one explained anything to him.

On the honeymoon, Frank found out that he couldn't consummate the marriage. (Frank was a very sensitive person and a gentleman, even though some people thought of him as being tough). It took almost two years to find out it was a vitamin deficiency. When things seemed to be working in July, the relationship wasn't any better. Jezebel was very demanding and expected Frank to give her material things that she wanted when she wanted them. Frank had to spend a lot of time on the road to make money. Frank was away in September on a business trip, so they were not together at all during that month. Frank was a little surprised when Jezebel told him that she was expecting their first child and the child would be born in June. When Frank and Jezebel shared with her parents that they were expecting their first child. Her parents came to their home and said to her, "How dare you bring that child into the world?" Frank couldn't understand why they would say that and asked her parents to leave. Frank thought that was an odd response to their daughter having her first child. Did her parents know something that Frank didn't know? Why would her parents say something like they did?

After the birth of their second child, Jezebel would go on business trips. One-time Frank didn't know where Jezebel was for several days. When Frank finally found out what hotel Jezebel was staying at, he called in the middle of the night and a man answered the phone. Another time Frank wasn't sure where Jezebel was, the doorbell rang early in the morning. When he went to the door, there was Jezebel passed out on the front steps. Frank brought her in the house and had to clean her up. She had been out partying, doing drugs and sleeping around. She begged him not to throw her out. He believed in the commitment he had made with her before God, and if she was willing to stay, he felt he shouldn't divorce her. Their two boys were very young at the time, and he was hoping that somehow, she would change her ways and that they could be a family. Shortly after this incident, Frank thought he had the flu. He wasn't feeling good, his body was aching, he was tired all the time and he even passed out. Jezebel was not very sympathetic about his condition and when he went to a doctor, he found out why. After having some test work done, Frank was told by his doctor that he had a low level of poison in his system. According to his doctor someone was giving him small doses of poison. When the doctor told Frank this, the doctor wouldn't let Jezebel in the office because Frank thinks the doctor suspected it was Jezebel. Frank and the doctor couldn't prove that it was Jezebel, so Frank was advised to be careful about what she offered him. What a horrible way to live, especially with someone who promised to love and care for you. Frank was a contractor and due to an injury, he found out that he would have to get back surgery. The day he went for surgery, Jezebel drove him to the hospital and dropped him off. How could she do that when he was having something as serious as back surgery? The marriage vows say in sickness and in health. That means when a spouse needs you, you should be there for them. Jezebel never came to see him in the hospital and Frank had to find his own ride home. His recovery was long and painful; he had to learn to walk again. During the time he was recovering at home, he started having the same symptoms that he had when he was being poisoned before. The verbal and emotional abuse that goes along with this makes it very difficult for a person to understand what is happening to them. To be married to a person who you know doesn't care about you, is a very painful thing to accept.

Jezebel was not committed to the covenant she made before God. She was too busy committing adultery to care about the part of the vows that say, "in sickness and in health"'. Jezebel's office job, is whereas she put it to Frank, found it socially acceptable to sleep around even though you are married.

It took approximately two years for Frank's recovery. It was a miracle that he was able to survive the poisoning and the surgery. Frank was not able to work and that caused more problems between them. Alice wondered," Was Jezebel just mad because Frank didn't die like she had hoped?" Alice wondered if Jezebel got the idea of poisoning Frank from something she watched or read.

God had other plans for Frank, that not the devil or Jezebel could change.

Since Frank couldn't go back to doing the work he used to do, he thought that if they bought a store together, he could run the store. That was something he could physically do at the time. Jezebel had an office job, so they were not usually in the store at the same time. When Jezebel decided, she did not want to work in the office anymore and wanted to own the business as sole ownership, she filed for divorce. This was in June 1990. Jezebel wouldn't let him sell the house, but after he signed the house over to her, she signed the house back to the bank and she moved out of the house, When Jezebel moved out of the house, she took everything in one day. She drove Frank to work that day but when he had gotten a ride home that night everything in the house was gone. She had the money to hire someone to move the furnishings out of the house and get a dumpster to throw out all his clothes. He was left with a few personal items and the clothes on his back. So, that left Frank homeless (the house was valued at approximately $300,000 and the store was worth approximately $700,000). If they were sold and if not, the store could make approximately $300,000 per year plus it had $47,000 in it that should have been used towards the support of the children until Frank was able to get work. It is a hard thing to get a job when you do not have any place to live (he also gave the car to Jezebel for the children), no car and you are recovering from surgery. What did Jezebel do with all the money that was in the store, and why did she continue to harass Frank when he was doing what they had agreed on in their divorce decree?

Two months after they got divorced, September into October, Frank was working at a lawncare business so he could have some money to live on. Frank was still working at the store as was agreed in their divorce decree in lieu of child support.

In September 1990, Jezebel had filed for modification, even though he was working in the store as agreed, the court allowed an amount of $175.00 per week to be put down as a child support payment. Frank was not made aware of this. At the same time Jezebel was getting the money she would have paid someone else to work at the store for the hours that Frank was working. Frank was only making $200.00 per week (outside of working at the store) because he was putting more time at the store that only Jezebel owned. Frank was able to get an apartment above a garage from a man whose wife was working part-time at the store. He had the apartment but spent more time at the store working up to midnight and then open at 4 am when the supplies would come in. Many nights because Frank didn't have a car, he would sleep in the back office. On August 15, 1991, a modification was awarded of $150.00 per week. Then on October 10, 1991, Frank was told he had to pay $200.00 toward an arrearage by October 11, 1991, and beginning October 18, 1991, he would have to begin paying $175.00 per week plus $25.00 towards arrearage. (Frank was only bringing home

$200.00 per week and working at the store and not being paid), so the court ordered him to be left with nothing to live on. Frank thought that he was doing what the divorce decree said, he didn't understand that this money didn't include the time he was putting in at the store and not getting paid.

This is how the arrearage started to build up. Frank could not afford an attorney. According to the Support Enforcement officer who had Jezebel's case, she told Frank that she could influence the judge to have everything go in Jezebel's favor.

Frank continued working at the store and Jezebel led him to believe that everything was all right, even though, she would demand more money than he was working off in the store. Frank thought the time he was putting in at the store was so he could get to see the children. The divorce decree required that he work at least 25 hours in the store, but he ended up working between 60 and 70 hours a week for $4.00 per hour.

Jezebel was supposed to be using the money Frank worked for towards the child support. He worked in the store for nineteen months. The time he worked came out to between $240.00 and $280.00 per week and between $11,520.00 and $13,440.00 per year from a man who ended up being homeless. He was giving money to a woman who was hiding money and then claimed he didn't give her anything for the time that he had worked in the store in lieu of child support. He never saw the money; he couldn't have a checking account because he didn't have an address.

When Alice spoke to an Attorney General, seventeen years later, he told her that Frank could have gone to the Labor commission within a two-year period, but of course, at the time nobody shared that with Frank (not even the attorney who had written up the divorce decree).

Jezebel should have been questioned regarding the fact that Frank had worked without pay, but the commission who decides on how to persecute us regarding child support felt that it wouldn't be fair to burden the custodial parent. Frank fulfilled what was agreed on. Jezebel and the Support Officer will be accountable for what they did. The courts should have done what was right under the circumstances, but they didn't. Frank was getting to see the boys every other weekend. He tried to hold onto the apartment so he could have a place for the boys to stay with him, but the apartment was costing him $400.00 a month. This didn't leave him much to live on because Jezebel would tell him he had to give her more money if he wanted to keep seeing the boys (that's extortion). Many times, this meant leaving him with nothing to buy food with, but he wanted to see the boys. Frank stopped working at the store in the beginning of February 1992, after walking in on Jezebel and her new boyfriend on the desk in the back office. He was wondering what the boys, who were only two and five years of age were doing in the front of the store unattended. He walked out and wasn't going to work there anymore. Jezebel told the landlord of the apartment Frank was renting from that Frank had abandoned her and the two boys. When the landlord confronted Frank, Frank told him it was none of his business what was going on between them. The landlord had hired Frank to do snow plowing for him but hadn't paid him for the work he had done, so Frank thought it would go towards the rent. The landlord then locked Frank out and threw all his belongs out. Now everything Frank owned was gone, even the handwritten slips that Jezebel would give Frank for the cash child support payments. Now Frank had no proof of the payments he made to take care of his children and Jezebel used that to her advantage.

In February 1992, Frank had started working for a man who owned a body shop and since he no longer had any place to live, he ended up sleeping in the body shop at night. One night it was getting very cold out, and the guy who owned the body shop felt it wasn't a good idea for Frank to stay there because it was extremely cold. Frank told him he had no place to go, the guy asked him "Can you call anybody?" Frank tried calling his older brother (his brother had his own business and at one time Frank had worked with him) and his brother hung up the phone on him. He called his brother back and said," A lot of good it did for me to call you to even ask for a job". Frank explained to him that he had no income and wanted to come back home and see if he could get some work and get caught up with the child support arrearage (that was wrongly put on him, this is what the courts are doing). Frank told his brother that he didn't know what else to do, his brother hung up on him a second time. The third time Frank called him back and said, "A lot of good it did me to call you, I might have well just walked out in front of a truck and then slammed the phone down. This is what this court is doing to the fathers who care about their children. The courts are putting these men in situations that make them feel so desperate that they don't see the point of going on. Frank stayed in the body shop that night with no heat and rat infested, he curled up underneath the desk. Not knowing if he would survive the night. Frank gave his life to Jesus Christ that night and, no matter how treacherous the Child Support courts became, Frank knew that God was with him through whatever they did. This was Frank's saving grace. The bible says in 1 John 3: 16-17-KJV "Hereby perceive we the love of God, because He laid down His life for us: and we also lay down our lives for the brethren. But whoso hath this world's good and seeth his brother have need, and shutteth up his bowels of compassion from him, how dwelleth the love of God in him? Frank started living on the street, he would sleep in the body shop whenever he could, instead of outside in the cold. Frank heard there was a warrant for his arrest when a marshal came to the body shop where he was staying. The marshal said that he had been looking for him for quite a while. Frank told the marshal that he didn't have any personal belongings. The marshal had compassion for what was happening to Frank (it's pathetic that there is no compassion in the Child Support courts, to bring a person down to this level and not care whether a person can handle what they are doing to them or not). The marshal told Frank he wasn't going to bring him in, and that he would show up in his behalf, but if Frank didn't show for this meeting, he would come and arrest him. Frank agreed to be there. On February 20, 1992, it was determined that the arrearage was $3140.0. The man who owned the body shop gave money to Frank to bring into court. Frank was working on a truck to fix up and sell to make some money to live on and pay for the child support. Frank was able to bring in $2400.00 and at the time it was determined that the arrearage was $740.00 Even though it was determined that Frank could make approximately $200.00 per week the court put $150.00 a week for child support and $25.00 towards arrearage, leaving him with $25.00 to live on. When the judge asked Frank why he hadn't been making any payments. Frank told the judge that he thought that he was paid up until February because of the time he had worked in the store. There was approximately $47, 000.00 that was left in the store that should have been used for the children while he was struggling to survive. He told the judge that he needed to buy himself some clothes because he was living outside and food. The judge looked at Frank and told him, "You have to pay your child support before you can think of those things." (This is coming from a man who is well paid and well fed and living in an expensive home.) This situation reminds me of the story of the rich man and Lazarus in Luke 16: 19 -3 1 KJV. There was a certain rich man, which was clothed in purple and fine linen, and fared sumptuously every day. And there was a certain beggar named Lazarus, which was laid at his gate, full of sores. And desiring to be fed with the crumbs which fell from the rich man's table; moreover, the dogs came and licked his sores. And it came to pass, that the beggar died, and was carried by the angels into Abraham's bosom; the rich man also died and was buried. And in hell he lift up his eyes, being in torments and seeth Abraham afar off, and Lazarus in his bosom. And he cried and said, Father Abraham have mercy on me, and send Lazarus, that he may dip the tip of his finger in water and cool my tongue; for I am tormented in this flame. But Abraham said, Son, remember that thou in thy lifetime receivedst thy good things and likewise Lazarus evil things; but now he is comforted, and thou art tormented. And beside all this, between us and you there is a great gulf fixed; so that they which would pass from hence to you cannot; neither can they pass to us, that would come from thence. Then he said, I pray thee therefore, father, that thou wouldest send him to my father's house: For I have five brethren; that he may testify unto them, lest they also come into this place of torment. Abraham saith unto him. They have Moses and the prophets: let them hear them. And he said, Nay, Father Abraham; but if one went unto them from the dead, they will repent. And he said unto him, if they hear not Moses and the prophets, neither will they be persuaded, though one rose from the dead.

This judge, like many judges and lawmakers violate God's laws and our Constitutional rights and are not giving us due process of law. Frank had no clothes no belongings. The children should have had plenty of money to be taken care of. Frank told the judge that Jezebel had harassed one of the places he had worked for before and they let him go. Jezebel would threaten to have the guy arrested because he had illegal aliens working for him. Frank had no proof of what Jezebel was doing, the courts would not hear what he was telling them. The judge is telling him he should have a full- time job and he could if Jezebel would stop calling and harassing his employers. Frank could never understand why Jezebel didn't want him to be with the boys and why she wanted him to be put in jail. Those were the two things she wanted, and the court system went right along with it. One job Frank was able to get was a part-time job at a bakery. Frank met someone who knew of a room for rent, and he stayed there for a while until

Jezebel found out where he was. Again, Jezebel was violating the divorce agreement. She hired someone to follow Frank (she had money for that and yet she continued to use the courts to get money from a man who was trying to do what was right and help with his children). She harassed and threatened the people he was renting from. When they couldn't stand her bothering them anymore, they asked Frank to leave. Jezebel did whatever she could to get back at him.

Frank then worked for a landscaper. Jezebel found out and the harassing and threatening of the employer started again. What Jezebel was doing was stalking him and if he did it to her, he would have been arrested. Jezebel went as far as blackmailing the employers because they had illegal aliens working for them. She would tell them to give her money so she wouldn't report them or fire Frank.

Frank started working at a marina around August 1993. Frank explained the circumstances about what was going on and what the courts were doing. The owner of the Marina offered Frank a small room to stay in and part of his job was to keep an eye on the marina. The owner paid Frank the money he needed to pay his child support.

When Jezebel found out where Frank was working, she got a child support officer to start harassing Frank. One day the owner overheard the Support Officer threatening Frank that if he didn't come in with a large sum of money, she had a judge that would make sure things would go the way Jezebel wanted it to go.

On page 2 of their divorce decree it stated: That the parties may and shall, at all times hereafter, live separate and apart free from all interference, authority and control of the other as fully as if each of said parties were sole and unmarried, and each shall be free to conduct, carry on and engage in any employment, business or occupation which to him or her shall seem advisable for her or his sole and separate use or benefit without, and free from any control, restraint of interference direct or indirect, by the other party, in all respects as if each were single and unmarried.

It is understandable why this was written but obviously Jezebel did not think it pertained to her. She did what she wanted because the courts interference in families allows this kind of behavior to happen. On September 7, 1993, the court modified the arrearage again and went back to 1990 when it had already been determined in 1992 that the total arrearage was only $3140.00. Frank had paid $2400.00 towards that leaving $740.00. So, the judge put the arrearage up to $17,410.00 when there was only a $740.00 arrearage. What the judge did was wrong! It is also wrong that the Support Enforcers can influence a judge's decision by giving them the wrong information. Now, Frank had this false judgment put against him. In November 1993, Frank's sister and father brought him back to the town where he grew up, so he could get back on his feet. Frank got a job delivering furniture. It was the only job he could get, even though he had had back surgery. His sister helped him get an apartment which happened to be near Alice. Frank would pass by Alice's apartment every day. Alice felt that she knew him from somewhere but couldn't remember from where or when. She had tried dating but there were not too many guys that were interested in having a ready-made family.

In August 1994, Alice was trying to get to a light that went out in her car. Frank saw her struggling and offered to help her. Frank's two boys seemed a little annoyed about having to wait while he was helping her out. This was one of the times they spoke. Another time they were talking about their previous marriages and at the same time they both said, "I'm never going to get married again." They both laughed because they said it at the same time.

In passing, Frank and Alice spent time together and eventually became friends. They both were struggling to get by, it helped to have someone to talk to. Frank didn't get to see much of his boys because of what the courts allowed Jezebel to do. Frank couldn't afford a car, so he borrowed his sister's car if he needed to go pick up his boys, who now lived forty-five minutes away. Frank would help Alice with her two children whenever and however he could. He was the first guy that she met that was a gentleman and seemed to have concerns for her and her two children. Alice had been praying for years for someone who would love her, and her two children and she believed she found that someone in Frank. Alice and Frank would take long walks together and many times Frank would join them for dinner. Alice didn't realize how little he was being left with because of the child support courts. Frank would help her with little things like doing the dishes which was a nice change for someone to offer to help with that.

The few things they did included the children. Alice's two teenagers and Frank's two boys when he was able to see them. They dated for what was said, "too short a time". When Frank asked Alice to marry him. Alice wasn't sure what to do, she really enjoyed spending time with Frank. Alice felt that her years of praying for a man who not only loved God but also had the room in his heart to help Alice with her two teenagers had finally come to an end. Alice longed for her family not to be broken and yet she knew it would not be easy. Her children were used to it being just them in their mother's life, and even though, her son had wanted a dad, he didn't like it when Frank would tell them they needed to listen to their mother. Frank would back up what Alice would tell them to do. Alice never had help like that before, the children's father would blame her for whatever the children got into. Instead of giving her help and encouragement, he would tell her everything was her fault. It didn't take long for Alice to realize that Frank was the answer to the prayer that she had been praying. They were married by a Justice of the Peace. Alice's two children were witnesses along with her mom, sister and brother-in-law, two nieces, his sister and her husband and his dad. Alice remembers how nervous her son got because Frank was a little late. He went down to Frank's apartment to see where he was, and he wasn't there. Frank had walked to the florist to pick up a wedding bouquet for Alice and flowers for her daughter and boutonnieres for her son, her mom and for himself.

Frank and Alice were married in 1995 and shortly after that Frank had gotten hurt at his job of moving furniture, so then he needed to find a job that wouldn't be so hard on his back. He eventually found a job working in a senior village on small machines. Alice wasn't making a lot of money at the time so whatever she made had to take care of rent and household bills. Frank got behind on child support payments because of the time it took him to find a job and then wait to be paid. Jezebel had gotten remarried about four months after Frank and Alice, but she felt the need to continue to harass him. She gave him a hard time about the boys and his visitations. She eventually brought him back to court. Frank had to hire another attorney with money they didn't have. And so, the court visits began.

According to Frank's divorce attorney, the Support Enforcement officers function is to compile the information (they are not supposed to do anything else; they are supposed to remain neutral in the circumstance). The Support Enforcement officers, in this case, sided with the custodial parent and will go to any extent even to have someone follow you, by the state you live in. The Support Enforcement is also using other state employees to get involved. Even the marshals that are hired to serve the papers don't understand why they are going to this extent; it is not a crime. According to one Attorney General, he said that it is a crime, but it is not a crime. It is not a crime to be poor in this country, so according to the government, it you can't pay what they have decided how much you should pay for child support (even if it leaves you homeless and without food or shelter) you are committing a crime.

A Support Enforcement officer told Alice that she could not speak to a judge because that would be influencing the judge. The Support Enforcers tell judges what they want the judges to hear, so the judge makes a judgment based on what they are being told. The custodial parent might be saying things that are false and they do not have to prove what they are saying. Unlike the non- custodial parent, who must have proof for everything.

If someone is making $100,000.00 a year with a steady income and doesn't take care of their children that is shameful. 1Tmothy 5:8 KJV But if any provide not for his own, and specially for his own house, he hath denied the faith and is worse than an infidel. If you are struggling and can't find a job it is wrong for the courts to harass you and put false arrearages on a person and make it look like they are deliberately not taking care of their children. This is what this court is doing. To me what the court is doing is a crime, it's called extortion. If the custodial parent has a job and can take care of the children financially without the help of the other parent, then the court should not be allowed to interfere if the other parent is trying to help support the children the way they can. Just because it might not be the way the custodial parent wants. In some cases, if the non-custodial parent has issues that has the custodial parent concerned for the safety of the children, then this is where families should work together to help not the court system. The courts interference allows the custodial parent to stop visitations to get back at the other parent and causes the financially struggling parent to have to find money to hire an attorney so they can see their children. This is not right. By the time the case gets to court, the judge will say that since the non-custodial parent hasn't seen the children, the judge shortens the visitation. Instead of fining the custodial parent, who prevented the visitation from happening. Not taking more time from the non-custodial parent who wants to spend time with the children.

In Jezebel's case she had a full-time job and the store (Frank signed over to her), so she had two incomes. She would give Frank a hard time about spending time with the boys. She was in contempt of the visitation orders many times and the courts didn't make her accountable for it, so she kept doing it until Frank couldn't afford to go to court to get visitation back. She also would drag him to court for modifications because she wanted more money.

In child support courts when you go before a judge and that judge makes a ruling it is not like a regular court where you get a jury, a trial or you can get a bail out. You get sent straight to prison. Your Civil and Constitutional rights have no effect in this court. They don't just put you in jail, they put you in prison. If a judge makes an unfair judgment, according to a Senator that Frank and Alice spoke with is this: You can file a complaint. Of course, that costs more money (which you don't have because the courts have bled you dry financially). Then you must hire an attorney when you go into review the complaint. The government has this all figured out. They can do what they want, and we must come up with money to fight what they do wrong. They make laws to protect themselves and they claim they are working for us. Almost everything will come up in their favor, so where are our rights?

The courts left Frank with $25.00 a week to live on, how is that right? It isn't right.

In 1996, Frank's attorney argued the fact that the court had put child support payments that were too high for what he was making, but the courts didn't care. When Frank was working at a furniture store, he was making $1160.00 a month and they were making him pay $656.00

per month for child support. Basic child support from a schedule from 2005: a person making $290.00 per week should have only been paying $97.00 per week and they were making him pay $175.00 per week. In order to change the court order, he would have had to hire an attorney and put in for a modification and even then, there is no guarantee that the courts would grant it. The courts usually didn't. The courts were making him pay what would be equivalent to somebody who was making $500.00 per week.

What he was paying was almost fifty percent of his income. He was being left with $115.00 per week. There is no justice in the child support court system and no due process of law.

Alice shared with me that the last time Frank had to fight for visitation with his boys was in January 1997. It was after Jezebel had tried to have Frank over-medicate the youngest son.

Frank and Alice had gone to pick up the two boys Friday after Thanksgiving in 1996. The youngest boy had a very bad cough. Jezebel had given Frank some medication that she told him he had to give to him. When it was time for bed the boy started giggling and laughing because of all the medication that Jezebel had given him. Jezebel had told Frank to give the boy more medication before going to bed, but because Alice had worked in a pharmacy and taken a pharmaceutical course in college, Alice felt that they shouldn't give him anymore of the medications. Especially when there was a handwritten note (with Jezebel's handwriting) on a box of Nasacort. The note said put four squirts in each nostril. Alice remembering from working with a pharmacist, that Nasacort shouldn't be used on children under the age of twelve (Frank's youngest son was only nine years old). The instructions on the box also said only one squirt in each nostril. Alice felt Jezebel was trying to get Frank to over medicate the child. Alice couldn't imagine what kind of a mother would do something like that to a child, but then Jezebel did try to poison Frank, so nothing really would surprise her what this woman was capable of. And yet the courts thought she should have custody of these children. Whenever the youngest had a cold, he was given a cough medication with codeine, he was only nine years old. He stayed back one year in school; he probably had a hard time functioning with all the medication he was put on for a cold. When Frank and Alice brought the two boys' home on that Sunday, you could tell Jezebel was angry because the two boys were doing good. Jezebel wouldn't let Frank see the boys for their next visitation with him. Frank had called the doctor on Monday and the doctor told Frank that he hadn't prescribed the Nasacort for the younger boy. She blocked him from his visitations and then it took another month before Frank could get a court date to get to see the boys again. Here was another time when she denied Frank his visitation and he had to hire an attorney again to get to see the boys again. Jezebel violated an order and Frank and the boys ended up paying for it because the courts allow this to happen. When the custodial parent is the problem. When Frank finally got to see the two boys, the oldest son said, "It wasn't my mother who wouldn't let us see our father." Frank had to explain that if it wasn't their mother who prevented them from seeing him, then why did he have to go to court to get visitation again? The older boy started having a fit and wouldn't believe what Frank was saying. Frank then showed the older son the court papers. His oldest son was 12 years old and understandably it was difficult for him to believe his mother would lie to him. Frank just wanted him to understand it wasn't that he didn't want to see them. What a terrible thing to do to children. To lie and tell them that their father doesn't want to see them. A parent who would do this just to get back at the other parent is wrong, but the courts don't care. This is not in the children's best interest.

Frank and Alice did not have a lot of money. The courts were taking so much from them. When they had the boys with them both families would go for walks and hikes together. They lived in a small apartment because that's all they could afford. Jezebel didn't like the fact that the boys would enjoy their time with their father and his new family. One time, the younger son told them that when they got home their mother would interrogate him and she wouldn't leave him alone until he lied and told her what she wanted to hear. Alice couldn't imagine what lies he would tell her, just to get her to leave him alone. What Jezebel was doing was wrong, but the courts don't want to get involved in that. Then they shouldn't be involved in micromanaging the finances of the non-custodial parent either, in order to live financially. Because Jezebel was blocking Frank's visitation with the boys and making him have to keep paying an attorney in order to see the boys (Frank just ended up writing to the boys). Jezebel never let the boys see the letters that Frank wrote to them. A child support officer told Alice that the oldest son had written a letter to his dad and the letter had refused on it. Frank would never do that to the boys, but Jezebel would.

When Frank was in court in November 2005, Jezebel informed the court that the older boy is bi-polar. Frank was never informed of this. The judge even asked Jezebel why she didn't bring this up before. Frank was not able to hear the excuse she used. The only reason Jezebel mentioned this was because both boys were emancipated (she was trying to get the court to make Frank pay her for the son for the rest of his life, claiming he was disabled) and according to the law in 1996, Frank should not have to pay anything else to her even the false arrearage that was put on him. Of course, the law was changed after that, and Frank wasn't informed. This is one of the other games the court plays. They change the laws and don't inform the non-custodial parent, but the custodial parent seems to get the information. This way the custodial parent keeps dragging the non-custodial parent back to court making them spend money they don't have instead of using it for the children.

Frank found out through social media that the oldest son was working doing lawncare.

Frank did not get to see his boys for nine years because of what the courts allow. Then the courts allowed Jezebel to drag Frank back to court because she wanted the false arrearage that was put on him, a week before the youngest turned eighteen years old. This shouldn't have been allowed. It was bad enough that he didn't get to spend time with the boys, but then to make him pay money. How can you put a dollar amount on the time he lost with spending time with his children? Again, the courts don't care what's going on it is all about them keeping their jobs and all about money, not the best interest of the children. Frank didn't have the money at the time, so the judge was saying, "Where is your 401k, where is your savings, what do you own?" Some people struggle financially but the courts don't care. Some people don't have a 401k, savings etc. The judges do, the support enforcement officers do because they have good jobs and work for the state. These people can't understand that not everybody has it as good as they do. The only thing that Frank and Alice owned was a house that needed work and they couldn't get any money out of it at the time. The judge had Frank put in handcuffs like a criminal then he was taken away. Alice stood up and said to the judge you can't do this. The court bailiff shoved Alice and made her spin around and a young man sitting on the bench caught her. As Alice left the court room, she asked the judge," Where am I supposed to come up with the money?" There is no justice in this system. You can't get bailed out, you don't get a trial, just a misguided judge who has no compassion and claims they must follow the law. This law is wrong and violates our constitutional rights. The reason they don't have a trial is because the court would be found out for the treason that is committed in this court to American citizens. The only way Frank and Alice were able to get through all of it, was their belief in God and knowing that God would never leave them or forsake them, no matter what happened. Not saying it was easy for them to trust when this court takes away everything that you were taught about living in a free country. This court makes you feel as though you are in the wrong country, but you didn't move.

CHAPTER 3

Child support/ Arrearage

Who makes the laws? How are
these laws hurting families?

The people who make the laws regarding Child Support are the people whom we have put in the positions they are in. Governors, Senators, and Congresspeople. These are jobs that are well paying ones. The problem is this: they make laws for many of the people who don't have well- paying jobs. They sit around not being able to figure out how come people can't take care of two separate homes, like many of them are able to.

The so-called formulas they come up with are for combined incomes of both partners and how many children there are (the parents are no longer living together, so how is it fair to combine the incomes?) These formulas were taken from a book that Frank got from a Sheriff who brought him papers from the court. For example: if the non-custodial parent net income is $310.00 and the custodial parent is making $500.00 per week. This formula combines the incomes which equals $810.00, The way the formula goes the non-custodial parent is required to pay $260.00 per week for 2 children. Now that would leave the non-custodial parent with approximately $50.00 per week to live on. Who could possibly think this is just and fair? Then our lawmakers came up with another tactic. They made a law that the non-custodial parent must be left with $145.00. Maybe we should reduce our lawmakers pay to that and see how long they would survive. Matthew 7:12 KJV Therefore all things whatsoever ye would that men should do to you, do ye even so to them; for this is the law and the prophets.

If the custodial parent is having a difficult time they can turn to the state for healthcare, housing and food, if they need it for the children. There are no resources for the non-custodial parent, whom may have been left homeless or have taken their lives because they have been left with not enough to take care of their basic needs. How can lawmakers feel what they are doing is right? Whose eyes are they right in, theirs? If the non-custodial parent made $3000.00 per week and their spouse made $1000.00 per week the combined income would be $4000.00. For two children the cost for the non-custodial parent would be $636.00 per week. This would leave the non-custodial parent with $2364.00 per week, so this formula works for the financially well off, but not for the average and lower middleclass person.

The problem with the law is this: the state and government are using the inability to pay child support as a means of putting people in debtors' prison which is against our Constitution. Bankruptcy laws were made because you cannot put a person in prison for a debt, but Child support is apparently above that. That violates everything this country was founded on.

The other problem is this: the child support laws change so much and so often that even if you have something in your divorce decree, the new law can override what was agreed upon and the custodial parent can drag the non-custodial parent back to court for modification whenever they want (many times, at no cost to them, but a big cost to the non-custodial parent). This costs money to have to keep hiring an attorney. What is the point of having an attorney when you get a divorce if the courts can change whatever was agreed upon between two people?

When you go to Child Support court, the judge can make a judgement that's wrong because of what the Support Enforcers are telling them. This information which could be wrong such as claiming the non-custodial is making more than they are. The judges claim they won't change what another judge has ruled on and yet they change what the divorce judge ruled on. In one case a judge approved that as the non-custodial parent's salary increased, the child support was to increase. Another judge said that can't be done, but it was something that was agreed upon by the divorcing couples. What kind of game is this court playing with people's lives and the lives of their children?

I was taught in school that the laws were made by the people and for the people. We are also taught at one time, "Do unto others, as you would have them do unto you". Our lawmakers do not live by the laws they are making regarding the family. All the laws they make, don't apply to them, because if they did, they wouldn't make the ones they make because they couldn't live by them and yet they expect us to live by them. If they could put themselves in the difficulty of a divorce (where one person is unreasonable) then they shouldn't interfere in the private lives of other people. According to the Constitution, they are not supposed to. It gets more and more obvious that the people in charge of this country have forgotten what they are there for. Their greed has consumed them so much that they have lost the ability to perform the jobs that they were given. To work for the American people and not fill their pockets while draining the life out the Americans who remember why their ancestors came here in the first place. To get away from governments controlling their lives.

The average income person cannot afford to go to court as often as they end up being pulled into child support courts. The court room seats are full of hurting and bitter people. The judge doesn't have time to hear each case, so the judge cannot possibly make the right decision regarding each situation. Then who suffers, certainly not the judge or the support enforcement officers, but the people who are already suffering from the situation that has occurred. The courts look at it like the people who are broken, struggling emotionally, psychologically and financially are not paying the outrageous amounts they put on them on purpose. The court was not involved and should not be involved in the family before or after divorce (only when violence occurs, any man that would hurt a woman and children and any woman who would poison her husband does not deserve the gift that God has given them. Not that any of us deserve anything.) The family is God's, what God will do to the people who don't do what's right is going to be worse than anything man can come up with. It's God's place to judge us for what we do, not man's place when it comes to the family. If the courts can't do it with basic fairness, then they shouldn't get involved in the family. Fairness and due process of law is what our Constitution gives us as citizens of the United States, and our politicians are supposed to uphold it and they are not.

The following information is not everything written in a booklet titled, "Child Support and Arrearage Guide" (effective August 1, 2005) but I tried to address what was important for people to see how our representatives come up with the laws. I will share my comments at the end.

The primary purposes of child support and arrearage guides are:

- (1) To provide uniform procedures for establishing an adequate level of support for children, and for repayment of child support arrearages, subject to the ability of parents to pay. To make awards more equitable by ensuring the consistent treatment of persons in similar circumstances.

- (2) To improve the efficiency of the court process by promoting settlements and by giving courts and the parties guidance in settling the levels of awards.

- (3) To conform to applicable federal and state statutory and regulatory mandates.

Basic principles:

The Child Support Guidelines are based on the Income Shares Model. The Income Shares Model presumes that the child should receive the proportion of parental income as he or she would have received if the parents lived together. Underlying the Income Share Model, therefore, is the policy that the parents should bear any additional expenses resulting from the maintenance of two separate households instead of one, since it is not the child's decision that the parents' divorce, separate, or otherwise live separately. The Income Shares Model reflects presently available data on the average cost of raising children in households across a wide range of incomes and family sizes. Because household spending on behalf of adults for most expenditures, it is difficult to determine the exact proportion allocated to children in individual cases, even with exhaustive financial affidavits. These economic studies have found that the proportion of household spending devoted to children is systematically and consistently related to the level of household income and the number of children. In general, the economic studies have found that spending on children declines as a proportion of family income increases, and a diminishing portion of family is spent on each additional child. Based on this economic evidence, adjusted for this state's relatively high-income distribution, the guidelines allow for the calculation of current support based on each parent's share of the amount estimated to be spent on a child if the parents and child live in an intact household. The amount calculated for the custodial parent is retained by the custodial parent and presumed spent on the child. The amount for the non-custodial parent establishes the level of current support to be ordered by the court. These two amounts together constitute the current support obligation of both parents for the support of the child.

Intact households are used for the estimates because the guidelines aim to provide the children the same support they would receive if the parents lived together.

Federal regulation for the Title IV-D child support enforcement program (45 CFR 302.56) require among other things that the guidelines review process include a consideration of economic data on the cost of raising children. The schedule percentages included in the 1994 and 1996 guidelines were based on economic data on child rearing costs gathered in a study mandated by the Family Support Act of 1988 (P.L. 100-485, section 128). The study was conducted by Dr. David Betson of Notre Dame University, through the University of Wisconsin Institute for Research on Poverty. Dr. Betson used data from the U.S. Bureau of Labor Statistics 1980-86 Consumer Expenditure Survey for his research. The commission notes that the identification of spending categories for the development of estimates of expenditure on children does not translate well into an obligation for parents to spend specific portions of their own income, or support payments received from the other parent, on categories of items for their children. As stated earlier in this preamble, spending on children and adults in families is inextricably intertwined, and the commission specifically rejects a requirement on the part of the custodial parent to provide for an accounting of how support payments, or the custodial parent's portion for the presumptive current support obligation, are used to provide for the child. An accounting requirement would represent an unreasonable administrative burden on courts and administrative agencies and would be extremely intrusive for custodial parents. The commission does not believe it is appropriate for the government to micromanage family finances. On the other hand, where it can be shown that a parent's failure to provide for a child rises to the level of neglect, it certainly is appropriate for individuals to enlist the help of appropriate court for agencies to assess the appropriateness of a custody changes or other measures to ensure the child's welfare. The commission emphasizes that it is the obligation of both parents to contribute to the support of their children to the extent of their ability, as defined by the guidelines and ordered by the courts.

Rothbarth estimator

Economists determine the average household spending on children by comparing the expenditures of two households that are well off economically, one with children and one without.

Adjustments for some states:

Some states have an income structure that is much higher than the national average. This fact, in the commission's judgement continues to warrant an upward adjustment to the Betson/Rothbarth percentages, for the following reasons:

(A) In some states a household can be expected to spend about the same percentage of income on children as a nationally representative household with a lower level of income because of the state's income distribution.

(B) Households with lower levels of income generally spend a higher proportion of their income on children.

Percentage decline as income increases

(A) Economic evidence establishes that the proportion of household income spent on children declines as household increases.

(B) Decline at all income levels. Some states pre- 1994 Child support guidelines built in a decline in the percentages beginning at the $750 combined net weekly income level.

Low-income adjustments

(A) A historical perspective. One of the continuing themes that surfaced throughout the Commission's review process was the challenge of striking an appropriate balance between the interests of parents and children in the setting of a child support award when one or both parents of extremely limited means. On the one hand is the child's interest in sharing equitably in the parent's income. On the other hand, is the low- income parents need to retain sufficient income to provide for his or her own subsistence, in order to permit such parent to play a positive role in the child's life. Previous commissions have resolved this inherent tension in various ways. For example, the 1994 and prior commissions established an income level below which a non-custodial parent would have no responsibility for child support payments.

(B) Low-income adjustments in the new schedule. The present commission recognizes that in low-income families where the parents reside in two separate households, there will be inevitably be immense financial pressure on both parents to maintain themselves and their children.

Nonetheless, the commission returned repeatedly in its deliberation to a concern for the best interests of the child.

No obligation for parents with less than $50 net income. The commission determined that child support obligations for non-custodial parents earning less than $50 per week net income should be eliminated, despite its adherence to the principles enunciated by the 1999 commission regarding imposition of obligations in low-income cases. Parents with such extremely low income are in truly desperate circumstances, and their first concern, even before the payment of a child support obligation, understandably is their own economic survival.

Arrearage guidelines

Section 46b-215a of this state General Statutes requires the development of guidelines for orders of payment on arrearages. Such guidelines are to be based on the obligor's ability to pay. The commission interprets the statute to apply only to the determination of periodic payments, and so does not address in the regulations the determination of lump sum payments, which determination remains subject to the discretion of the judge or family magistrate.

Simplicity

The commission believes that the arrearage guidelines should be simple to understand and apply, and accordingly continues to base the arrearage payment on a percentage of the current support order.

(1) Percentage of current support
    The commission determined that (20%) of the current support order continues to be a reasonable percentage to apply toward the reduction of accumulated child support arrearages in most cases. It has accordingly retained this percentage as the general rule, subject to limitation described in subdivision (4) in this subsection of the preamble.

(2) Arrearage payment when there is no current support order.

    (A) 20% if the child for whom the arrearage is owed is an unemancipated minor, or over age eighteen.

    (B) 50% if the child for whom the arrearage is owed is deceased, emancipated or over age eighteen. The fifty percent amount was selected because in the situations described, the obligor's current support obligation will have ceased. (In Frank's situation the judge made him pay $10,000.00 towards his false arrearage that they had at $13,000.00 when both boys were both over 18 years of age. Frank should have only paid 50% which would have been approximately $6500.00)

(3) Limitation on amount of arrearage payment

Basing the arrearage payment on the current support order automatically introduces a test of the obligor's ability to pay. Nonetheless, the commission recognizes that further protection is required to assist obligors in meeting their own self-support needs. It has accordingly retained in these regulations the provisions whereby no more than 55% of obligor's net income may be taken for the total of all current support and arrearage payments.

(4) Special rule for low-income obligors

The lower percentage (Which is 10%) is

Intended to assist such obligors in meeting their own self-support needs while at the same time conveying the important message of the primacy of the child support obligations.

(5) Arrearages owed to the state and a custodial parent.

The commission has retained the provision for a single arrearage payment order under which payments are to be distributed in accordance with federal requirement. As under the 1999 guidelines, the order is to be repayable to the custodial parent until such parent arrearage is satisfied, and then to the state.

(1) In general

The commission recognizes that keeping the deviation criteria to a minimum serves the stated guidelines purpose of ensuring consistency and promoting settlements. It also finds, however, that due regard to the best interest of the child, as well as fairness to the parents, requires a description of the specific circumstances in which the presumptive support amounts may be inappropriate or unjust. The commission considered case data reported from the automated system maintained by the state's Title IV-D child support agency in arriving at the regulatory amendments.

(2) Applicability

The new language permits agreements to set supports amounts that deviate from the presumptive amounts but requires that such agreements cite specific deviation criteria and factual bases to justify any variance.

(K) The guidelines commission and review process

(L) Statutory authority and membership

The commission for Child Support guidelines is established under section 46b-215a of this state's general statues. The commission is charge with establishing guidelines to ensure the appropriateness of child support awards and for reviewing and updating such guidelines every four years. The commission consists of eleven members. The Chief Court Administrator, the Commission of Social Services, the Attorney General, and the chairpersons and ranking members of the joint standing committee on judiciary all serve in their place. The Governor appoints a representative of the bar Association, a representative of legal services, a person who represents the financial concerns of child support obligors, and a representative of the Permanent Commission on the Status of Women.

After reading the guidelines I see hypocrites, one minute they are saying they should not interfere in the family and then they describe how they will interfere with the family. Since the children are entitled to receive a portion of the parent's income, this is ridiculous. They say they are not micromanaging the family and yet they are. When a couple gets divorced, they come to an agreement and then a judge makes a judgment regarding the agreement, what Is agreed upon should not be changed because of Child support guidelines. The Bible says a child should Honor their mother and Father. It doesn't say the child is entitled to their parents' money. The commission also thinks that the average person can afford to support two households. Most people are just making it with one household. People that are well off or paid well because they have a good job might be able to do that. So that tells me that the people involved in making these laws are financially well off because they could afford two households.

The laws they are making are not basic fairness and intrude on how we take care of our children by telling us what the state and government are requiring us to have, money wise, to spend on our children. My concern is if the government has found a way to intrude on broken families and violate the Constitution and Civil rights, who is to say they won't find a way to intrude on the intact families like some countries do.

The courts do not understand what is going on in a relationship, how is their place to judge what a couple is doing after a divorce. When a couple gets to the point of divorce the relationship is broken in so many ways. It can be very difficult to "work things out" with a person who is totally unreasonable, and has been, that's why the marriage failed.

People who marry people who have not put God first in their lives eventually come to understand the part of being unequally yoked. What is sad, the unreasonable person has no fear of God because they will lie to get what they want. They will try to make it look like it is the other person that is the problem, but they are really the problem, and the courts choose to believe them.

What the courts have done is put a price on a child like an object or a car or house payment. There should not be child support in a divorced couple unless one of the spouses are abusive or have addiction problems that would cause the children to not have their basic needs taken care of, and even at that it should be taken care of at the point of the divorce.

In one of the estimators, they compared households without children to households with children. How can you compare one with children and one without children?

When a judge tells a man that he had to pay child support before he eats and has clothes to wear because he is homeless and is struggling to find a job is not treating another person with respect or concern for their well-being.

The commission thinks a non-custodial parent should continue to pay for a deceased child. To me this is not right. Isn't it enough that a child has died nevertheless expect the non-custodial to continue to pay for a child that has passed away? Anyone who would expect someone who is dealing with the loss of a child to continue paying for that child, should not be put in charge of judging what other people do. In most cases people are not financially well off by the time their children reach the age of 18 years. Especially those who have been harassed by the support enforcement officers and the courts. In the case of Frank, his ex-spouse harassed him so much and denied his scheduled visitations of his two boys. That he ended up having to choose not to be a part of their lives because he couldn't afford going to court. The judges didn't care that his visits were denied by his ex-spouse and didn't care that he couldn't afford to keep hiring attorneys to help him get his visitations back. The commission and the courts are not concerned about the best interest of the children from what has been done.

The courts change the laws, and the non-custodial parent is not informed until a sheriff comes knocking at their door with a subpoena for court.

The commission should be charged with treason for violating our Constitution and our civil liberties with the laws they are making against the family.

Some of the laws consist of:

1. If you cannot pay child support you will be put in jail or prison, without a trial. This is not due process of law. This is also debtors' prison, which is also against the Constitution. That's why we have bankruptcy laws. How can a person pay a debt when they are in jail or prison?
2. The state will take away any licenses the non-custodial person has. If they do this, how is the person supposed to make a living? The state will also make the person sell any equipment they have, how are they supposed to make any money when you take away their means of making it?
3. The state puts a bad mark on your credit report, so you can't even borrow money to pay off an unjust amount of arrearage that was put on you. Some companies won't hire you because they don't want to deal with the government harassing them. A support officer said the reason for this: You might become a flight risk.

4. You can't get a passport, because they are afraid you will become a flight risk.

5. The government takes the tax refunds that are due to you, if you owe any arrearage.

The laws that are being made are violating our civil liberties and hurting families. I see more violence in the homes because our government has turned our pain of divorce into a profit. The government has turned our children (who are free gifts from God) into bargaining tools that turn people more against one another. People who are already struggling with betrayal, heart pain, separation from another partner/spouse. Some people have turned to killing/kidnapping the other spouse or children because they don't know how to deal with the pain and the fact that they can't financially afford the lawyers, the court proceedings, the bullying by the custodial parent and or the Support Enforcement officers. These are matters of the heart and government as stated in our civil liberties, do not belong in our private lives. The commission does not have the right to judge or make guidelines for us. God will be the judge for how we took care of the gifts He has given us. If our court system and our government kept God in this country (which this country was based on) then we would not have as many problems as we are having with the family. If God were first in our lives, then love would follow, and people would be less likely to judge one another and be willing to help those that are struggling.

A few cases that I have recently read about- a mother was arrested for leaving her children in a car while she was at work because she couldn't afford child- care. So instead of helping this woman get child- care, the government says "in the best interest of the children" we will throw their mother in jail and give the children to a stranger. I can't imagine how desperate this woman must have felt to leave her children in the car. This is not loving our neighbor. This woman was working to take care of her family. Our laws would rather put someone in jail who is struggling then to help them.

A man who was left with only $50.00 a week to live on because the courts felt it was "in the best interest of the children" to take so much away from him that he couldn't afford to take care of himself that he took his life. How is this in the "best interest of the children"?

The commission, support enforcement and the judges who rule over this court, will be accountable before God for what they are doing to people and the pain they are causing them.

The Child Support Guidelines are violating our rights to raise our children in accordance with our parental beliefs and telling us how much we need to spend on our children according to their statistical findings.

Custodial/Non-custodial
How is it determined who is the better parent?

According to Divorce-Father's Rights by George Coppolo, Chief Attorney Judges use the "best interest of the child" standard in awarding custody of minor children. In any family relations case, including dissolutions, the court is authorized to require an investigation of the circumstances of the child and family and cannot if it orders one, dispose of the case until the investigation report has been filed (CGS 46b-6 and 7). The investigation can include the child's parentage and surroundings; his age, habits and history; the home conditions habits and character of his parents; an evaluation of his physical and mental condition; the cause of the marital discord; and the parties' financial ability to provide support (this violates our Civil Liberties). The court may also appoint counsel for any minor child when it deems it to be in the child's best interest. (CGS 46b-54)

It would be in the "best interest of the child" to be with the more stable parent. My definition of a stable parent would be the parent who knows what commitment is. A parent who is abusive or commits adultery does not know what commitment is and would not be able to give a child a stable home life. He who is faithful in that which is least is faithful also in much; and he who is unjust in the least is unjust also in much. Luke 16:10 KJV.

A 1990 state study using 1980 and 1984 data found that mothers were granted physical custody in 84.3% of the cases sampled from court records (What does this mean? All of these studies are statistics that have been taken by looking into who received child custody. It doesn't tell you if the person who had custody did what was in the best interest of the child).

The article from Divorce-Father's Rights- states that disputes about violation of custody orders are resolved by bringing the matter to the attention of the Superior Court, which has jurisdiction over such disputes. The court can use its mediation services to help resolve disputes, but ultimately it decides what the facts are and can modify a custody order or hold parents in contempt of court for violating custody orders.

It didn't work this way for Frank, when Jezebel would deny him visitation with the boys. Frank would have to pay an attorney to go to Family court. Each time he would go to court, which usually took a month to get to be seen by a judge. Jezebel was never held in contempt for denying him his visitation to see his boys. The judge would reduce the amount of visitation time because Frank wasn't being consistent with the visits. Jezebel was violating the custody order and the judge would allow her to continue to do this.

The court recommended Frank and Jezebel to go to mediation. The mediators and Jezebel attacked Frank's integrity and lack of commitment to the boys, and the inconsistency of seeing the boys. As was stated before, Jezebel was the one that was denying Frank his visitations, but the mediators didn't want to hear that. When Frank pointed out that the boys were getting along with Alice's children and that she should be included in the mediation. The mediators suddenly decided it would be too confusing for the boys if they spent too much time with them. Frank brought up the fact that Jezebel had a revolving door of men, even before they were legally separated staying in the house with the boys. That sounds like it would be more confusing and psychologically damaging for the two young children to see their mother sleeping with different men. So, when the mediators started looking at what she was doing, she didn't like it and wanted to leave. This was the only mediation they had, and nothing was resolved. The mediators felt the visitations should be shortened for Frank. How could they come up with this assumption when they don't really know what has been going on and why Jezebel was denying visitation. Jezebel did not like the fact that the boys enjoyed their time when they were at Frank and Alice's house. Their home was peaceful and less stressful. The boys would say that it was not that way at their home. Frank was treated unfairly; he tried the best he could to be there for his boys and the court allowed Jezebel to pull her games to hurt the boys. The children are the ones that get hurt when one parent has the agenda to get back at the other parent for whatever the reason is. What Jezebel was doing was not in the best interest of the children.

The article from Divorce-Father's rights also stated that someone who believes the Superior court treated him unfairly can appeal the decision to the Appellate Court, which can review the transcripts and other court records, receive written Arguments from each side in the form of legal briefs and hear oral arguments. Some disputes can ultimately reach the State Supreme Court. What nobody tells you is this, it all costs money to hire an attorney to fight these decisions. The Judges are given information by people (who don't know the real circumstances of the situation) who make assumptions usually by believing the parent who has custody of the children. Because according to the Commission the custodial parent can basically lie about the situation and be believed because it would put a burden on the courts and administrative agencies to investigate the truth and would be intrusive for the custodial parent (basic fairness is the same for both, the only way to find the truth would be to look at both parents, and that is invading our privacy which is against our Constitution).

The best interest of a child is being loved and being with a parent that wants that child. Not because the parent is calculating how much money they can get from the other parent. This just causes more struggles within an already bad situation. The children become caught in the middle and this is not "in the best interest of a child". The interference of the courts makes the situation worse in many cases. Especially in those in which the non-custodial parent is financially struggling.

Divorce Who Profits?

How to survive it

Whoever has been through a divorce, knows that they are not the ones to have profited from the divorce. The exception to the rule might be Jezebel. She got the house, the store, and got to take away Frank's rights to see the boys. She used the attorneys, courts, judges, mediators, support enforcement officers to get what she wanted, revenge on her ex-husband. Usually, the people who are suffering are the ones who were tossed aside because the one spouse got tired of working at the marriage or because they thought starting another relationship was an answer to their problem, instead of working on the marriage they were already in.

Divorce has the same symptoms as losing a spouse to death, only its worst. It's worst because when someone dies a natural death it's not their choice. When someone walks out it's their choice. When a divorce occurs, you can go through the same symptoms as a death, divorce is the death of a marriage. The symptoms can include fatigue, hollow or empty feelings in the chest and abdomen, sighing, hyperventilation, anorexia, insomnia, and the feeling of having a lump in your throat. The psychological symptoms begin with an initial shock and disbelief accompanied by an inner awareness of mental discomfort, sorrow and regret. These may be followed by tears, sobbing, and cries of pain.

Alice remembers experiencing these symptoms when she was living in the west. A woman, whose husband worked with Aaron, was concerned about Alice because she was looking so thin. She was experiencing the grief symptoms approximately six years before she became divorced. That is a long time to be grieving anything. So many times, she wanted to walk out, but she believed in staying and working things out. It's a hard thing to do when you're the only one looking at it that way. It takes three to make a marriage work and if God is not the center of it, it's hard for it to work the way God intends it to work.

The worst things got in the relationship the more Alice turned to God for answers. She would read God's word and trust Him to help. So many times, we pray for what we want instead of asking God for His will in our circumstances. We think we are doing what is right, and we think the answers we are choosing are the surest way to go, but sometimes our choices bring us right where we are. We argue with God and try to tell Him how to help us, but it is not until we truly let go and give it to Him and then the truth comes clear. Many times, we are being tested by God and don't understand the reason for it. Sometimes it is better not to question why, because not knowing why is how get through what we're going through.

Matthew 6: 25, 32b, 33, 34 KJV Therefore I say unto you. Take no thought for your life, what ye shall eat, or what ye shall drink; nor yet for your body, what ye shall put on. Is not the life more than meat, and the body than raiment? for your heavenly Father knoweth that ye have need of these things. But seek ye first the kingdom of God, and his righteousness; and all these things will be added unto you.

Take therefore no thought for the morrow; for the morrow shall take thought for the things of itself. Sufficient unto the day is the evil thereof. I know in my heart God knows better than we do. So many times, though, when you are in the middle of things that you don't understand it is difficult to find comfort. The Bible says in Psalm 147: 3KJV He healeth the broken in heart, and bindeth up their wounds. When the world is throwing so much at you, you often lose your focus. Your focus should always be on Jesus. There is a song that says, "Turn your eyes upon Jesus, look full in His wonderful face, and the things on earth will turn strangely dim. In the light of His glory and grace. This was written by Helen Howarth Lemmel in 1922. We do not understand what is happening to us, it is not just about us. God may be trying to get someone else to come to realize that they are heading in the wrong direction by what they are doing to someone else. God desires in 1 Tim 2:4KJV Who will have all men to be saved, and to come unto the knowledge of the truth.

Someone once shared this saying with me, it goes something like this: Bread cast on the water comes back to you. The good deed you do today may benefit you or someone you love at the least expected time. If you never see the deed again, at least you will have made the world a better place, and after all isn't that what life is all about? Ecclesiastes 11: 1KJV Cast thy bread upon the waters; for thou shalt find it after many days. This is like that saying.

CHAPTER 6

Debtors' Prison
How you end up here

This is how you end up in debtors' prison.

1. A judge puts an unfair amount of arrearage on you (without due process of law.)
2. You spend the time until the children reach 18, going to court being harassed by the custodial parent and the government. (The government takes your tax returns because of the information given to them by the state you live in, whether it is correct or not.)
3. Your credit and character are ruined by one judge's decision.
4. You can't borrow money to pay back the false arrearage put on you because the state and government put it on your credit. They ruin your credit by saying you owe the state the debt. The banks won't loan money to you because they know that you can't file for bankruptcy if it is child support, but you could if it's a bank loan.

5. You can't get a good job because of what they put on your credit report. Most companies do not want to deal with the state harassing them

6. The laws change and you are not notified, and what was agreed by you and your ex-spouse is ignored. The state allows changes to be made so the non-custodial parent is always being pulled into court at their expense. Taking so much time in court can affect your job if it keeps happening. Frank was told in 1997 that once his boys turned 18 the law has no jurisdiction, but when the law changed Frank was not informed. After not seeing his boys for over 9 years, his ex-wife pulled him back into court a week before the youngest child turned 18.

7. Support Enforcement influences the judges, the officer that worked on Frank's ex-wives case told him that she could influence the judge's decision, and everything would be in favor of his ex-wife and that's exactly what happened.

Frank was followed by people his ex-wife could afford to hire and harass him, and then eventually the state started following him.

The Support Enforcement officers are supposed to remain neutral, according to one of Frank's attorneys but that is not what is really happening.

Frank and his attorney were told by a Support Enforcement officer that the judge will not accept your proposals, even if they are reasonable and fair. So, the Support Officer makes you feel as though he/she knows how the judge is going to rule, even before you bring your proposal to the judge. Frank and his attorney had told the Support officer that Frank would need at least until September to get the house in the condition it needed to be in, in order to get an appraisal from the bank. The Support Officer told Frank and his attorney that the judge would not go for it, so Frank and his attorney were under the understanding that Frank would have to come back and give a monthly report on the progress of the house. Frank and his attorney offered to make the $10,000.00 arrearage as soon as he could get the money from the bank and in the meantime, Frank would continue paying the $50.00 per week payment that was ordered in November of 2005. The judge had stated at that time that this didn't belong in her court because both children were over eighteen and yet she put the judgement against Frank anyway. The attorney Frank had in November 2005 agreed to help Frank but because Frank couldn't come up with the full retainer at the time, the attorney didn't inform him that he could have appealed the judgement within 21-day period.

Financially Frank and Alice were struggling, so Alice tried contacting the Attorney's General office regarding the fact that this arrearage shouldn't even be there because of what was agreed upon at the time of Frank and Jezebel's divorce. Alice was told it would be investigated and was to be assigned to one of their attorneys (who was hard to get a hold of) and when the attorney finally got back to Alice, the attorney said they couldn't help. In the meantime, Frank was not able to pay what the court had ordered. He couldn't find work. The house they were living in was using electric heat and the bills were running between $500.00-$600.00 a month to heat the house. It left them little to live on. In April 2006, Frank was told that a sheriff had a warrant for his arrest. Frank was finally able to find some work and had to give everything so they wouldn't put him in jail. The banks wouldn't loan them money because of what the state put on his credit. They were in a no- win situation with no way out. Finally, Alice was able to borrow $7500.00. As I mentioned earlier according to the Child Support laws once the children were over 18, Frank should have only been required to pay 50% which would have been about $6500.00. They called the Support Enforcement officer and asked if Jezebel would accept the $7500.00 because this was all they could come up with. According to the Support Enforcement officer Jezebel refused to accept that amount. So, Frank knew he had to get another attorney, he had to use $1500.00 of the $7500.00 for a retainer, and then there were a few liens on the property which equaled approximately $4000.00 for work that needed to be done on the house. This left them with only $2000.00.

When Frank and his attorney went into court in June, this is when they proposed that Frank would settle by paying Jezebel $10,000.00 but only with the understanding after they were able to get the house finished enough so that they could get the money out of the house.

Frank thought that he could get enough work done on the house, so they could get an appraisal done, but as it turned out the banks required more done than they could do. They had taken the balance of the money to do the work on the house, so they were left with no money and no way to get anymore. Frank tried getting from family, but no one would help. Alice went to several banks trying to get loans, but all refused, even the bank they had their mortgage through. The Support Enforcement officer knew the condition the house was in because he had pictures of the house. Taken either by Jezebel or the state people that were following Frank. According to Jezebel, Frank shouldn't have a cell phone or a truck. Someone also took a picture of a machine on the property which Jezebel told the Support Enforcement officer was owned by Frank (which was not true). When Frank knew he wasn't going to be able to get the work done by July 2 to be ready for an appraisal before July27th, he called his attorney. Frank's attorney told Frank that he was going to be out of the country and that he would not be able to be with him on July 27th. Frank's attorney assured him that because he was up to date on the $50.00 payments that he was not in contempt, but Frank would have to show up on that date to answer for the continuance. Frank told his attorney that if he didn't come with him, they would put him in jail, but the attorney assured him that everything was taken care of, and he just had to show up.

7

The Court – Where
justice is not served

On the outside of Child Support court is a list of names. When you find your name, there is a number next to it. You then go into the courtroom and give that number to a clerk at a desk. When Frank told the clerk his name and number, the clerk said, "I see you have a continuance filed, what date would you like to return, August 24 or August 31. Alice heard Frank tell the clerk, August 31. He asked if he could leave, and he was told that he would still have to go before the judge. Frank sat next to Alice, and then the Support Enforcement officer came out (before the judge came out) and told Frank that if he didn't have the $10,000.00 today, that he was in contempt, and would be put in jail. Frank explained that his attorney wasn't there and that he had filed a continuance. The Support Enforcement officer said that there was no continuance, and Frank said the clerk showed it to him. The Support Enforcement officer than went into the judge's chambers. The following is a summation of the transcript from the day that Frank's Constitutional rights were violated, and he was put not into jail, but into prison with no due process of law.

When the judge came out of her chambers, and the case number was called the Support Enforcement officer stated: Your Honor, this was a continuance from June 15th of '06, at which time the defendant was represented by private counsel. There was an agreement and a Court order entered into for a lump sum payment of $10,000.00 to be paid today and the balance arrears to be waived. The balance of 7/24/06 is $13, 075.69 (which was a false arrearage) My understanding is that counsel is not present. He was going to be filing a request for a motion for continuance, I do not see a motion in the file (and yet the clerk had just shown it to Frank that morning). For the record, Ms. Jezebel is expecting a $10,000.00 payment today as ordered by the Court.

The judge asked for Frank's situation and Frank tried explaining to the judge that he and his wife were in the process of trying to get the house to the point that they could refinance the house. Frank explained to the judge that his attorney was out of town and had told him that a continuance was filed and that because Frank was current on the weekly payments that were agreed on and because both he and his attorney understood this was just for the court to know that he was working on the house to get the money as was agreed through the refinance.

The judge wanted to know where Frank's attorney was, and Frank didn't really know. The attorney had just said he was out of town. Frank asked for the mercy of the court, he was working on getting the agreed amount. (Even though he should not have had to pay the amount they were telling him he had to pay according to the commission it should have been 50% of the false arrearage they put on Frank).

Jezebel then had the nerve to complain about how long she has waited, and the judge even acted like her time was more valuable than Frank's and Alice's time. The judge didn't care that Frank didn't see his two boys for nine years because of Jezebel. The judges don't want to hear what the custodial parent does or is doing. Jezebel wanted her money and she wanted it right now. This is the kind of person Frank had to deal with through their whole marriage.

When Frank was trying to explain that he was working to get the money. The judge started interrogating him about his personal expenses, which had been required to be filled out before.

Then the judge started asking if his bills were getting paid and when Frank said yes. The judge acted as though he should have not paid his bills and brought in the money to take care of this. In other words, according to this judge, Frank should have had his car repossessed and not been able to work and have his house taken away due to him not paying just to settle this debt.

Then the judge violated Frank and his attorney by appointing another attorney just so Frank would have representation so that the judge could do what she ended up doing. (Putting Frank in prison and violating his rights).

When the court appointed attorney spoke to the judge, he told her that he had checked into the continuance, and it was filed on July 11 but because of a clerical error it didn't find its way to the judge. This attorney also requested the continuance based on the fact that it was filed properly

The judge then said that she doesn't usually accept something that is contingent and then made Frank and Alice wait around until 2pm. At that time, the attorney asked if the judge would consider the motion for the continuance, and the judge said absolutely "no". Even though, the continuance was acknowledged.

The judge said if it's not in her file (even though it was acknowledged by the woman when Frank had entered the courtroom) then she won't grant it.

Then when the court appointed attorney questioned the Support Enforcement officer suddenly there was one faxed to them, but the judge never got it. So where was the justice then and what chance did Frank have when the people who are supposed be in charge are playing games with other people's lives. Was the continuance sent in by Frank's attorney purposely conveniently lost or was the judge telling the truth and really never saw it?

According to the court represented attorney for Frank the continuance was filed and had the date that it was filed.

When the court appointed attorney asked what the grounds were for the continuance, the Support Enforcement officer had a copy and the attorney read it. It explained that Frank's attorney would be out of the country when Frank was supposed to be in court, so the attorney requested a continuance for a later date. It said that the defendant is current with the payments he was told to pay and is in the process of refinancing his house for a lump sum settlement. At the time Jezebel was acting Pro se and the attorney was not able to contact her for consent.

The judge was being unreasonable and wouldn't accept the fact that there had been a continuance filed and acted like Frank should have known to check with his attorney to make sure it was filed. How would the average person know that they are supposed to check on the attorney that they paid to do a job and was under the understanding that they know what they are doing? It was also brought up to the judge that one had been filed two weeks prior to the second one that was sent into the Support Enforcement office. According to the judge even if your attorney files the continuance you are supposed to call the court to see if it was granted. The Support Enforcement officer acted as though they are the ones in charge but if your attorney doesn't do it the way the judge claims it should be done then you're the one who loses. Support Enforcement claims they told the attorney he must send it to the clerk's office so it can be seen and granted by the judge before you go to court.

What was discussed between Frank's attorney and Support Enforcement was an agreement to give Frank time to get work done on the house so that he could get the money but conveniently the Support Officer only had in his notes (nothing about what was discussed just that Frank was supposed to bring the money in on a particular date, and today was the day). Of course, his notes didn't contain the $7500.00 that was offered and refused by the plaintiff. She felt she should have all the money that she should not have gotten, because of all the money she caused Frank to waste on attorneys. She kept dragging him to court and trying to make him give her more money. He couldn't see his boys for nine years because of what she did (the courts don't care about that)

When the judge questioned Jezebel about what the order was and if Frank was paying, and that he was paying what the order was.

When the judge asked Support Enforcement how Frank had been paying. Support Enforcement said poor until they got involved the year after Frank and Alice had gotten married.

Which was a lie because Frank had hired an attorney who argued that what the court had put on Frank to pay was an unfair amount but the judge at that time would not change and, they were garnishing his wages at the time.

The attorney representing Frank said I also notice that the contempt citation the delinquency was $886.00. (This is what Frank's attorneys had argued about years ago. The large amount put against him was a false arrearage put on him by the state. This is what the Child Support Courts are doing to people).

IF the judge knew the law, then she should have known that because the children were over the age of 18 years of age that Frank should only have had to pay 50%. That's why the attorney was questioning the amount of arrearage.

All the judge cared about was that Frank didn't come in with the full amount then she questioned why he didn't come in with any amount. Even though, Alice was able to find a bank that would loan them money. The judge wouldn't accept it to be brought to the court the next day because the bank was in another part of the state that they could get the money from.

The clerk's office got the file but because the judge didn't get it she denied the continuance even though it wasn't the fault of the attorney but the clerk's office.

Then Jezebel starts asking why Frank can't pay the large amount when he has the money to pay for his car and house. (Frank worked for her and that money should have used in lieu of child support and she knew it). He also paid her with cash and the receipts were thrown away.

Then the judge made Frank and Alice sit around just to see if she would grant the continuance after saying she wouldn't grant it earlier.

When the judge returned to court the attorney for Frank explained that he had spoken to Frank's attorney and the attorney was also under the understanding that the court date was a report back date and as long as Frank was current with the payments he was paying and to report progress on how close he was to getting the refinance money from the house.

The judge listened to the tape and according to the law Frank should not have had to make a deal for any amount. According to the amount the judge quoted as an arrearage the amount should have only been 50% because of the age the children. Which should have only been approximately $6287.85. What kind of game do these courts play? There was no mention to the judge at any time about the $7500.00 offer that Jezebel refused according to the Support officer

The judge couldn't understand why Frank couldn't just use a credit card or just get a regular load. Alice and Frank were in debt and had used what credit cards they had so they just could not walk into a bank and get a loan for $10,000.00. Frank couldn't get any because his credit was ruined by child support putting a mark against his credit claiming he owed the state money. (His ex-wife was not using the state's money she had a job).

When speaking with the Support Enforcer in a back room. The Support Enforcer told Frank and his attorney that the judge wouldn't go for the date they originally wanted to ask the judge for. When you have Support Enforcers who are supposed to be neutral and they lie to you and tell you the judge won't go for what you need to do to take care of something, what are you supposed to do? Frank explained that he couldn't have an appraisal on the house until certain things were completed.

The judge said that if it was not said in front of her and it wasn't on the tape that it didn't count. What counted was what was recorded in the courtroom. The judge also said that the lender wasn't moving quick enough for her. (If the state didn't interfere by putting something against someone's credit, especially saying the person owes the state money, then they would be able to get a loan to pay off the debt). The attorney conveyed that Frank's attorney and Frank understood this date to be a report back to date and not a date to have the full amount. Then the judge went back to questioning Frank on his finances and expenses again.

The judge started making fun of the attorney and Frank because they didn't understand what the judge was saying about the fact that the money was expected to be paid on this date. According to the court appointed attorney the arrearage was only $886.00. Even though Alice was able to get $700.00 and the attorney was saying he was in compliance with a weekly amount that was set on him and that the contempt against him was only the $886.00. The judge said that was irrelevant and wouldn't accept the amount Alice was able to get.

Frank's attorney said: In one way it shows that his good faith of trying to resolve this matter. In representing it was everybody's understanding that this was a report back status as to the refinancing.

The judge said: It wasn't everybody's understanding. It wasn't support enforcement's understanding. It wasn't my understanding. The only person whose understanding it was is the person facing jail today. What do you have in the bank? (again, invasion of privacy).

Again, the judge asked him where he was getting the money from and then when Frank said a credit card. Then the judge started in on the financial affidavit. The judge threatened him with jail, and it would take the $10,000.00 to get out (extortion and a violation of his rights).

Frank and his attorney wanted the Support Enforcement Officer to swear to tell the truth what was discussed in that back room and of course he didn't. The Support Enforcement officer just told the judge what his notes said. (of course, he is not going to admit to the lies he told Frank and his attorney about the judge not accepting the September date that they had originally wanted).

When Frank's attorney asked if Jezebel was present in the meeting. She said she was, but she wasn't. She not only lied about being present in the meeting, but she also said she understood she was supposed to get the money today.

The judge then told the attorney that Frank was facing incarceration and that if he couldn't bring the money in that he should have requested a later date. (As was stated earlier the Support Enforcement officer said the judge won't go for it).

The judge started badgering Frank about why he didn't ask her for September. (Like it would have made a difference, this judge already had it in her mind she was going to put him in jail, no matter what was said). Then the judge told Frank he better decide if he wanted that attorney to come back with him on the next continuance date. That sounds like she was going to accept the continuance date.

Then when the attorney asked for a continuance date, the judge said no, and started asking about his 401K and how much he was making and if he was employed. And then started again on what his bills are and if he is paying them.

Then the Support Enforcement officer questioned him about who owns the vehicles. What most likely would have happened if Frank owned the vehicles the court would have taken it away from him then he would have no way to get to work.

The judge called it crafty business because Frank couldn't purchase anything because his credit was ruined by what the courts put against his credit. Frank's wife Alice had a good job at the time, and it was through her good credit was why they were able to buy what they bought. (The judge was mad because she thought she was going to be able to take his vehicle away from him). This judge was badgering him and telling him that because he doesn't own anything he should be paying what was put against him instead of paying the bills that he had agreed to take care of before Jezebel started harassing him after not seeing his two boys for over 9 years.

The attorney representing Frank tried to explain to the judge that because of the arrearage against him the banks wouldn't give him the loan that's why it was in his wife's name.

Then the judge told Frank that he needed to have $2000.00 by 1pm.

At 1pm when court was back in session. The attorney told the judge that Frank was able to obtain $1000.00 and would be able to get another loan for $2000.00 more but would not be able to bring that amount until the next day.

One minute this judge acted like if Frank brought in some money that it would be okay, then the next minute she wasn't accepting anything he had to offer. Then she had the tape played again and the attorney did say that the refinancing would take one to months. That's why the attorney and Frank thought this was just a status check on how things were going with the refinance.

The attorney then mentioned that the continuance was put into the court file.

The judge ignored him and then Jezebel was requesting receipts for the work being done on the house

The attorney repeated It was also the point with the one-to-two-month financing. That's what goes in sync with what the attorney thought it was a report back or a status conference.

The judge said that because the motion for continuance wasn't in her file, she was going to deny it.

Alice had to run around looking for a bank to give her the money hoping that the judge would accept what they could get. It was hot and she was tired. When she saw Jezebel on the court steps. She said to Jezebel are you happy now? You are getting want you wanted. So of course, Jezebel had to tell the judge that Alice had come up to her and shouted at her. Alice didn't go up to her they were passing on the stairs to the court.

The judge looked like she had crawled out from under a desk. When she came into the courtroom her hair was all messed up. The other times they had been in court, the judge's hair was just so. Alice knew that unless she could come up with the $10,000.00, Frank was going to jail, and she would have no way to get him out. Jezebel was so full of hate, she always wanted to keep Frank out of their lives because she didn't want the two boys to find out what kind of woman she really was. This was her opportunity to use the system to get back at Frank, because she blamed him for her inability to remain faithful in their marriage.

The judge said: I've made my decision. I thought about it on lunch hour. This was as clear as could be this morning to me, but I gave him the benefit of the doubt of a lunch hour break and maybe reconsideration. (Reconsider what, produce money out of the air, all of sudden pull the money out of his pocket and say I was only kidding I have the money). What a waste of time for everyone involved, she knew what she was going to do right from the beginning. She knew she had no right to violate Frank's rights, but she tried to make it seem as though this was the only way to solve this. (So, if a clerk makes a mistake that gives a judge the right to violate someone's rights) If there was a motion for a continuance, I usually would grant it (funny how everyone had the continuance but the judge).

Then Jezebel started in on wanting to see receipts.

When the attorney said they could provide them.

The judge said her request is denied and she ruled to have Frank thrown in jail (he was told by his attorney that all he had to do was show up, otherwise he would have brought papers showing his attempts to get loans and after lunch his wife was able to come up with $1000.00). The judge made the decision that Frank had the ability to pay the $10,000.00 when he didn't. Evidently this was a settlement on the entire arrears (which was another clerk's error and a judge put the false arrearage against Frank. Even though there was proof, no judge would overturn it) He's just failed to meet any burden of proof. He has brought no documentation as to any kinds of efforts made. And the court feels that he'll purge out if incarcerated and held to his end of the deal. So, he is going to be incarcerated. The purge is $10,000.00. He pays the purge he's out, and the case gets marked off.

When the prison guard grabbed Frank's wrist: Ow, ow, ow. My right wrist, my right wrist. (Frank had injured his right wrist just days before this, and the guards were trying to get his wrist together, but Frank's arm had so much muscle that his hands couldn't get close together and yet they yanked on his wrists anyway). Alice stood up and said," You can't do this". One of the guards shoved her and made her spin around and a man sitting in the front row caught her. Frank was taken away like a criminal and his rights were violated. The Constitution means nothing to this court. Alice couldn't believe what happened, she felt like she was not in the right country.

CHAPTER 8

When Rights are violated

Frank was not put in jail; he was put in prison. He didn't get a trial; he wasn't convicted of anything. Alice did not know where he was and where they had taken him until he called the next day. Alice asked Frank's family if they could help but no one could give her the money to get him out. A criminal has more rights than you have in Child Support court which should be called debtors prison court. They had no money to get him out. Alice couldn't even bail him out and yet a criminal can be bailed out. They had no savings, no 401k's, everything they had was put into fixing the house.

They bought this house because it was all they could afford. Two years after they bought the house (2003) if fell off its piers. They had to put whatever money they could to save the house. The bank they were working with at the time agreed to give them an equity loan. When they showed the bank, what was being done to the house. Then the bank withdrew the money they said they would give them to do the repairs. The bank said the house was in disrepair. They struggled financially to keep the house and the repairs needed to be done to the house.

The guards in the prison were furious because Frank should have never been put there. Frank's rights were violated by this system that claims it is in the best interests of the children. This was created by lawmakers which violate our Constitution and who are supposed to follow the Constitution.

Frank has allergies to foods, the food he was fed was horrible. They gave him a shot, which he was not sure of what it was. He slept in a large room with criminals around him in a bed that was like a banana boat because the prison was overcrowded. No wonder our prisons are overcrowded when you put people in prison because they can't pay a debt along with murders and drug dealers. Isn't that why bankruptcy courts were created?

Even under the circumstances, Frank could feel God's presence in the prison. People thought he looked different than he did, some thought he was a different race, the guards called him "'Big guy". A young man who was in prison because he happened to be in the wrong place at the wrong time stayed close to Frank because the other prisoners seemed to be afraid of him, but Frank shared God's word with them and many seemed interested.

Our lawmakers have created laws that allow two things that can't be put into a bankruptcy court. One is child support and the other is student loans. Both deal with children and goes against your credit and ruins your credit so that you can't borrow money from another bank to pay it off because the banks are afraid you will file for bankruptcy, and they will lose money.

Frank was put in prison on a Thursday, Alice didn't know where he was until he called on Friday. On Sunday, Frank was told if he didn't get out by Monday, they were going to ship him to a prison in another state.

Frank was in prison (not jail) for five days, until Alice's family member was able to give Alice the $10,000.00, they needed to get him out. Isn't that extortion?

When Frank finally got out, he was sick for months because of what he was exposed to. He was told by a doctor that he was having problems with his liver. Frank's health was put at risk because a judge didn't do the right thing. The judge could have granted the continuance until September. The clerk's office or the attorney made a mistake and the judge made Frank suffer for it. A year later, Frank found out that the judge who had put him into prison was arrested for DUI. These are the kind of people who can't even run their own lives right, stand in judgment of other people and violate their rights. At one point Frank had asked for mercy from the court but of course that wasn't in the transcript and of course he didn't get it. Apparently, the judge denied that also.

Romans 2:1 KJV Therefore thou are inexcusable, O man, whosoever thou art that judgest; for wherein thou judgest another, thou condemnest thyself; for thou that judgest doest the same things.

This judge judged Frank stating that he did not keep his end of a deal. The judge got into a motor vehicle under the influence. Did she know that driving while under the influence is against the law and yet she did? From things I have seen, judges are attorneys and apparently attorneys are above the law.

The Child Support Enforcement has gotten out of control. The laws that are made violate our Constitution. The Constitution speaks of our rights to privacy regarding family and yet our states and government are violating these rights with the laws that they make.

People should take care of their own children, and according to our Civil liberties it is not the governments place to interfere. There are women who are so bitter that they will use the system to get back at their ex-spouses. This was such the case with Jezebel, she was the one that committed adultery and destroyed the marriage and yet she had the nerve to go after Frank for what she did. She had a job and yet she could get a free or an attorney at a lower rate. She could pay for a private detective to follow her ex-husband (which according to their divorce decree she was violating that by what she was doing) and made false accusations (bearing false witness) about what he was doing and what he owned. That shouldn't be allowed but that's what happens when a government agency thinks that they know what's in the best interest of the children. They don't live with the people, they don't know what is really going on, so they shouldn't be allowed to interfere. The system doesn't even look at what the custodial parent is doing even when there may be abuse.

The courts have turned this into a hostage situation, then they wonder why people turn to whatever means they feel they must do, because the courts interfere and won't listen to both sides of what's going on. Our Politicians don't care, and they won't' do anything because they are a part of the making of these laws that are hurting the citizens that put them in their position.

It shows me what happens when a government takes God out. First prayer was taken out the schools, so that the children who are being raised by parents who don't believe in God are never exposed to learning about God. Then people wonder why there is so much violence happening in our schools. I pray for the lawmakers who think they are in charge and don't understand that God gave them the positions they have, and they will be accountable before Him when their time on this earth has ended. The lawmakers need to ask themselves, "Do I want to be judged the way I am judging people who are in difficult situations?" In Romans 12:19 KJV Dearly beloved avenge not yourselves, but rather give place unto wrath; for it is written, Vengeance is mine; I will repay, saith the Lord.

God will vindicate the righteous and He will punish the wicked. God judges with perfect mercy and justice.

CHAPTER 9

Child Support or Extortion,
What is the difference?

I looked up these two words through online dictionaries.

Support- to provide for or maintain by supplying with money or other necessities.

Children need more than just money, but the courts have decided that this is the only way. In the state, where Frank and Alice live, if you don't have the means to pay child support, they won't allow you to take care of the children in the way that you are able to. The state thinks that because the state workers (who are paid well) can afford two homes, then everyone can afford two homes. But that's not the case and they are the ones who are making the laws that are hurting people.

According to our Civil Rights: Protected as parts of due process are the rights to marry, to have children, and to raise them in accordance with parental beliefs. The Government has passed laws that interfere with a parent's right to raise their children in accordance with parental beliefs. Just because a divorce occurs, that should not allow this change. When you get a divorce, agreements are made between the two parties involved, and what is made an order should not be allowed to be changed by another judge.

The government and states are interfering in many families, with the Department of Children and Family, this department should be one that is helping people, instead, you hear of them taking children away from their homes. In many cases this is uncalled for. There are many people who need help with raising their children. Many families are struggling financially, years ago families and the churches were able to help families. Times have changed, the cost of everything is so high. Families don't live as close to one another as they used to. Some jobs take people away from where their families live such as the military.

Many people have to work two and three jobs to support a family and sometimes that is not enough. Our government chooses to give money to people who are not willing to work, free health care and housing. While the people who are willing to work struggle to make ends meet.

The way they come up with the amounts of support to put on the non-custodial parent is unjust. To add two incomes, as if two people were still living together, and expect the non-custodial parent to pay half of what the total amount is, is unfair and not right. It would be more just to make the non-custodial parent to pay a portion of what they make alone, not combined income. The people that make six figure salaries are the only ones who can afford the way the law is made. The average working person can barely afford one home or place to live. Even at that, I don't think it is our governments place to put a price on a child, when God has given that child without a price

Extortion –The criminal offense of using one's official position or powers to obtain property, funds or patronage to which one is not entitled.

The states, government, and support enforcement are using extortion as a means of getting money out of people. Even when a judge has ruled wrongly, or a clerical error has occurred such as the case that happened to Frank, is extortion. He was paying on an order, he was current with his payments, he offered what money he was able to come up with and yet a judge decided (because the judge has money) that he was holding back money from the court. He was trying to get the money whatever way he could legally acquire it. All he was asking for was a little more time. The only way to get money was to get an appraisal on the house but the bank kept saying the house was not finished enough. He was financially in debt. The judge had him put in prison until he paid the debt. He had to sit in prison with people who had trials by juries and had been convicted of crimes. The criminals had more rights than he had. Child Support Court is basically judge and jury which is not fair, but they know a jury wouldn't convict someone for not being able to pay something because that violates our rights. He was exposed to people who don't know what personal hygiene is, he witnessed in prison a man die from a bullet wound in a plastic bag like his life had no value. Our government is now dictating to us that if we can't pay what they determine as what we should be paying to take care of our children, we are criminals. Bearing false witness or perjury is a crime which Jezebel did. She told the judge that Frank owned equipment Which he didn't, she claimed he was working in places that he wasn't on a legal document, she lied about the arrearage she knew he had paid the money but because the receipts were thrown away by what she did he had no proof, she violated Frank's visitation rights, and nothing was done to her. Why was nothing done? Because according to Child Support it would not be fair to look into what the custodial parent is doing. If these things are not addressed about the custodial parent, then there is no basic fairness, which is against our Constitution.

When our government is allowed to make laws that are against our Constitution, then it is time for the people to stand up and say something. These laws regarding Child Support need to be changed or eliminated. The money we save by eliminating the positions for support enforcement and the hard-hearted attitudes of the judges that they have over these courts. We could feed and clothe and help shelter any family in need, in this country. Giving people help is better than kicking people when they are down. People in divorce situations and matters of the heart are the people that need our help, not laws that make criminals out of struggling souls. Teach people how to be better parents. Teach our children not to be so promiscuous. Keep God in our schools, our government and our courtrooms.

Have judges that believe and fear God, so they can have the wisdom to rule wisely despite what laws are made, especially the ones that violate the Constitution. When a government chooses to make laws regarding the family, like they have. There is no difference between support and extortion because either way the non-custodial parent loses, and many times so do the children. Especially when the custodial parent has learned to use the system to get back at their ex-spouses. How is it to the benefit or the best interest of the child, to know that one of their parents was put in prison because they didn't have money to support them? In Frank's case, financially he had to stop seeing his children because Jezebel keep bringing him to court and denying his visitation rights. He had to stop seeing his boys because he felt it was better to use his money to pay the child support then to waste his money on attorneys and use his time to work instead of wasting it in a courtroom, which was what was happening.

A person could lose their job from being pulled into court as often as Frank was. Just because attorneys and judges have nothing else to do then be in court because that's their job. The rest of the world must make a living outside of the courtroom.

What is the level of recourse when justice has not been served?

The people whom we elect, tell you that if something has been done wrong, you can file a complaint against the judge or attorney or officer.

Frank and Alice have investigated this and let me share with you what they found out. If you file against a judge, you will eventually need an attorney to represent you, if you cannot afford one you might as well not even waste your time or money. The people whom we have put in authority over us have come up with so many laws to protect themselves and the judges, that as an average person you could not afford the legal fees it would take to fight their misjudgment of a situation. Most of the time you'll be told the judge only ruled on the information that was given to them. So, if an attorney or support enforcement officer gives a judge the wrong information the judge will make a judgment based on that.

Our government is not looking out for the people they are supposed to be serving. They have figured out how to line their pockets with the hardworking Americans money (they call it taxes) and they freely give away our money to people who can work but figure; why work when you can get things for free. This is for those with that mentality- Nothing is free- someone has to pay for it. If you're not contributing to do your part, then you are part of the problem. 2 Thessalonians 3: 10KJV For even when we were with you, this we commanded you, that if any would not work, neither should he eat. The people who continue to allow the government to support them and their children are the reason why the government feels it's their place to interfere in the family.

Frank was told that he could file a complaint against the judge for what she did to him (violating his rights to a trial and putting him into prison). A continuance had been filed, it was in the court, a clerk showed it to Frank. Either the judge lied, or support enforcement didn't show it to her, or as I've heard attorneys say she was having a bad day. If a judge is having a bad day and is going to violate a person's rights, then maybe they should stay home that day. According to the attorney Frank was not in contempt, he was paying what he was told to pay, he just wasn't able to come up with such a large sum of money. So, this judge put a citizen in prison because he made the mistake of marrying the wrong person. A woman with no forgiveness, no mercy and vengeful. If marrying the wrong person were a crime, there would be more people in prison then there already are. If it's against a person's rights to be put in prison without due process of law, then why are our lawmakers making laws that do that when it comes to child support? To the politicians and lawmakers who are making these laws, do you understand that your time here is short? Do you not understand what the Bible says about what you should be doing? According to Matthew 7: 12KJV- Therefore, all things whatsoever ye would that men should do to you, do ye even so to them; for this is the law and the prophets. Would you want to live by the laws that you are expecting others to have to live by? Not everyone has a good paying job as politicians and attorneys have, so if you didn't, I doubt you would make the laws the way you do. Maybe we should reduce your pay so you can see how the rest of us live and struggle. When you die and stand before God you will have to answer how you treated your neighbor. How do you think He will respond when you tell him how you put them in prison because they couldn't afford to take care of their families the way you wanted them to, and how you put marks against their credit so they can't borrow money to pay the false arrearages you put against them? In Matthew 6: 12KJV And forgive us our debts as we forgive our debtors. Luke 7: 41, 42KJV There was a creditor who had two debtors, One owed five hundred denarii, and the other fifty. And when they had nothing with which to repay, he freely forgave them both. Proverbs 22: 27KJV If thou hast nothing pay, why should he take away thy bed from under thee?

I also would like to know how many people who are in prison that shouldn't be there? They tell us our prisons are overcrowded, well if the courts would stop violating our rights and putting people in prison that have not been tried and convicted of a crime then that would solve that problem, wouldn't it? When Frank and Alice would sit in the courtroom waiting for his number to be called, they saw men coming in in shackles, who had been in prison for child support, so their rights had been violated. One young man came into the courtroom in shackles and the judge mocked this young man by saying, I don't see anyone here for you. Alice felt so sad for him, wasn't it bad enough that he was in prison and in shackles and having to walk into a room full of people like that? Then to have a judge make fun of him for not having someone there for him. This is not loving your neighbor as yourself. I don't understand why they tell you to swear on the Bible to tell the truth. When God is not in the courtroom neither is truth, or love for one another. The child support court is the worst court Frank and Alice ever entered.

There is no recourse unless you have a lot of money to fight the court system. We the people need to send letters to our Senators, Governors, Congressmen, etc. And let them know that the states and the government should not interfere in marriages or divorces. The Constitution protects people's rights to live their lives as they desire. Whether the government agrees with it or not.

Frank's two sons were over eighteen years old, he didn't see them for nine years because of the way this court system allows a bitter ex-wife to use the children as a way of getting back at him. The judge said it didn't belong in her court and yet she made orders regarding a debt that should have been forgiven. What price can you put on not getting to see your children for nine years? For the children being told their father didn't want to see them.

Anyone who mistreats or neglects a child will have to answer to God. It is wrong not to take care of what God gives you and children are gifts from God.

What the Constitution says when it comes to the family and our rights

In the Text of the Constitution

A. Preamble

We the People of the United States, in Order to form a more perfect Union, establish Justice, ensure domestic Tranquility, provide for the common defense, promote general welfare, and secure the Blessings of Liberty to ourselves and our Posterity, do ordain and establish this Constitution for the United States of America.

B. Article 1

The Privilege of the Writ of Habeas Corpus shall not be suspended, unless when in Cases of Rebellion or Invasion the public safety may require it.

Comment: Citizens cannot be arrested and jailed arbitrarily except in extreme circumstances. (I don't consider child support an extreme case).

E. Article IV

Section 2. The Citizens of each State shall be entitled to all privileges and Immunities of Citizens in the several States.

Comments: The states must offer most fundamental legal rights to both residents and nonresidents of the state.

The Constitution protects many other civil liberties besides the freedom of speech and religion, **the right of privacy, and the rights of the accused.** Notable among these other liberties are freedom of assembly, freedom of association, the right not to associate, freedom of belief, and the right to petition the government-all protected by the First Amendment. **Protected as parts of due process are the rights to marry, to have children, and to raise them in accordance with parental beliefs.**

The Sixth Amendment guarantees people accused of crimes the right to a speedy and public trial. (Child Support Courts violate this, there is no jury involved just a Support Enforcement officer and a judge) Defendants in federal cases are entitled to be tried in the area in which the crime was committed, and both state and federal defendants have the right to have an impartial jury decide their guilt or innocence. The Sixth Amendment prohibits the government from prosecuting an accused person without first informing him or her of the nature of the charges against him or her. The accused has the right to "confront"-that is, to cross-examine witnesses who testify against him or her at trial. Those accused also have a right to subpoena(compel)supporting witnesses to testify in court and to have a lawyer assist in their legal defense. (Child Support Court doesn't allow the non-custodial parent to confront the custodial parents' false accusations)

The Seventh Amendment, which does not apply to the states, guarantees the right to a jury in some types of federal civil (noncriminal) trials. (The Federal Government has made a law to take tax returns from the non-custodial parent with an arrearage)

The Eighth Amendment states that the courts must allow most criminal defendants out of jail (in Child Support cases you are put in prison and can't get out until you pay. That is debtor's prison). Before their trial if the defendants put up a reasonable bail-a financial guarantee that they will come to trial. If a person is convicted of a crime, the government cannot impose unreasonable fines or inflict inhumane punishments.) What is "cruel and unusual" has no fixed meaning, and so decisions interpreting the clause are sometimes controversial. (Being handcuffed and put in prison with people who have committed a crime and have had a trial is cruel and unusual punishment.) The Supreme Court has generally held that a punishment that is wildly disproportionate to the crime is cruel and unusual. The Court has also upheld the death penalty against claims that putting someone to death, regardless of what that person did, is cruel and unusual.

The Ninth Amendment declares that just because certain rights are not mentioned in the Constitution that unlisted right is unavailable to protect individuals from the government.

The Thirteenth Amendment states that neither slavery, nor involuntary servitude (involuntarily under the power of another) except as a punishment for crime whereof the party shall have been duly convicted, shall exist within the United States, or any place subject to their jurisdiction. Slavery and peonage (A system by which debtors are bond in servitude to their creditors (or a custodial parent) until the debts are paid are illegal.

The Fourteenth Amendment-Section 1. All persons born or naturalized in the United States, and subject to the jurisdiction thereof, are citizens of the United States and of the State where they reside wherein, they reside. **No state shall make or enforce any law which shall abridge the privileges or immunities of citizens of the United States; nor shall any State deprive any person of life, liberty, or property, without due process of law; nor deny to any person within its jurisdiction the equal protection of the laws.**

The comment that follows this: Anyone born or naturalized in the United States is a citizen. All citizens are entitled to due process (basic fairness), according to the Constitution and Bill of Rights. Laws must be enacted and enforced in a way that treats people equally.

Conclusion

Since God made the family, which is the church, then the church should be the one that deals with the family issues not the government. Separation of church and state means the state doesn't belong in the church.

I was under the understanding that when someone takes a position of authority such as: The President, and the other public officials, they are supposed to uphold our Constitutional Rights and Civil Liberties when making laws. I do not see this happening, and We the People of the United States need to stand up to our rights and stop the laws that are being made to further hurt families already in crisis.

The government and the states are taking God out of our laws and decisions that are being made for the families. The family is something that God made, not our government or the states, therefore if you take God out of the government, you should take the family out of the government. Regarding marriage, the Bible says in Mark 10:9 KJV What therefore God hath joined together, let not man put asunder. Marriage is a covenant between God and a man and a woman, not the government. The only reason the state and government get involved is money- you must buy a license to get married. The government technically according to the Constitution is not supposed to interfere. When a divorce happens, attorneys must be hired to come to an agreement between the two parties, then they go before a judge to finalize what was agreed upon.

Democracy is defined in the American Heritage Dictionary as: A social condition of equality and respect for the individual within the community. Respect must be given and to be taught. In school our children are being taught that their parents can't spank them, that's teaching our children not to respect their parents. There are several places in the Bible where God tells us to correct our children. Proverbs 13: 24 KJV He that spareth his rod hateth his son; but he that loveth him chasteneth him betimes. Proverbs 22: 6KJV Train up a child in the way he should go; and when he is old, he will not depart from it. Without God in our lives, we cannot understand love, without love people are void of the understanding of God.

The laws that are being made regarding child support are more damaging to the family units and are not "in the best interest of the children". A parent in prison is not "in the best interest of the children". Fathers and mothers who have gone through divorce and tried to come to an agreement when they couldn't agree to work things out together in their marriage. Then to put them under laws that violate the Constitution and lack compassion for people who are already dealing with broken hearts and destroyed dreams and children that are hurting from having a broken home. Each member of the Commission will leave a legacy to their families of having made laws that violate our Constitution. If people could only understand that what we do in life echoes in eternity.

Our courts have taken out the Ten Commandments and yet they make people swear to God to tell the truth. When we took out the Ten Commandments, we took truth and God out of the courtrooms

> Leviticus 19:18KJV Thou shalt not avenge, nor bear any grudge against the children of thy people, but thou shalt love thy neighbor as thyself: I am the Lord.

> The questions the lawmakers or the Commission should be asking themselves as they make laws should be the following: Are the laws that are being made regarding child support showing love towards your neighbor? If you were struggling financially, would you want to be done to you, what you are putting on other people? Are your laws loving your neighbor or bringing them harm? God values people above possessions. You will have to answer to God for what you have done to your neighbor. In Matthew 23: 23bKJV and have omitted the weightier matters of the law, judgment, mercy and faith: these ought ye to have done, and not to leave the other undone.

> This country was started by God and for God. The child support laws are wrong. God gives us children freely without cost, what right is it for a state or government

to put a price on a child? The laws have taken a free gift from God and put a price tag on it. For our government to profit from the pain and suffering of our citizens is wrong. People who do not take care of a child are wrong. People who do not train up a child to love their creator are wrong. Taking prayer out of school and not keeping our focus on God, is what is causing the chaos we are now seeing. Children who are being abused and neglected now are the result of families who have had abuse in their households because God was not in them. Our children need to be taught in school and in our homes to be loving and caring adults.

Children come into this world as clean slates, what is carved into their characters is what is learned by their parents.

Galatians 6: 7-10KJV Be not deceived; God is not mocked: for whatsoever a man soweth, that shall he also reap. For he that soweth to his flesh shall of the flesh reap corruption; but he that soweth to the Spirit shall of the Spirit reap life everlasting. And let us not be weary in well doing; for in due season we shall reap, if we faint not. As we have therefore opportunity, let us do good unto all men, especially unto them who are of the household of faith.

Our lawmakers should be men and women who love God, who will show mercy on their fellow men and women. If someone does not know how to love, how can they show love. If our government got rid of support enforcement people and the judges who are ruling unmercifully over others, we would be able to help the struggling families. The ridiculous salaries that are being paid to these people could be put to better use.

The commands in the Bible are not suggestions and we as a nation will face the consequences of losing God's protection (which we already have gotten a taste of it on 911, shootings in our schools). We as a nation need to turn and repent and ask for God's forgiveness. 2 Chronicles 7: 14KJV If my people, which are called by my name, shall humble themselves and pray and seek my face, and turn from their wicked ways; then I will hear from heaven, and will forgive their sin, and will heal their land.

It is not the Commissions place to interfere with the family and make laws that hurt families more than help an already bad situation. It is our place to show compassion and mercy on one another and help one another, not make it a crime not to be able to pay an unjust amount of money put on by our courts.

Jesus summed up the Ten Commandments into two. The first four commandments are about our relationship with God: Exodus 20: 2-17KJV

1. I am the Lord thy God, which have brought thee out of the land of Egypt, out of the house of bondage.
2. Thou shalt have no other gods before me.
3. Thou shalt not make unto thee any graven image or any likeness of anything that is in heaven above or that is in the earth beneath, or that is in the water under the earth.
4. Thou shalt not bow down thyself to them nor serve them; for I the Lord thy God am a jealous God, visiting the iniquity of the fathers upon the children unto the third and fourth generation of them that hate me.

5. And shewing mercy unto thousands of them that love me, and keep my commandments

6. Thou shalt not take the name of the Lord thy God in vain.

7. Remember the sabbath day, to keep it holy

8. Six days shalt thou labour, and do all thy work

9. But the seventh day is the sabbath of the Lord thy God: in it thou shalt not do any work, thou, nor thy son, nor thy daughter, thy manservant, nor thy maidservant, nor thy cattle nor thy stranger that is within thy gates

10. For in six days the Lord made heaven and earth, the sea, and all that in them is, and rested the seventh day, wherefor the Lord blessed the sabbath day, and hallowed it

The last six are how we are to treat our neighbors

11. Honor thy father and thy mother; that thy days may be Long upon the land which the Lord thy God giveth thee.

12. Thou shalt not kill.

13. Thou shalt not commit adultery.

14. Thou shalt not steal

15. Thou shalt not bear false witness against thy neighbor

16. Thou shalt not covet thy neighbor's house, thou shalt not covet thy neighbor's wife, nor his manservant, nor his maidservant, nor his ox, nor his ass, nor anything that is thy neighbors

Matthew 22: 37-40 KJV Jesus said unto him, Thou shalt love the Lord thy God with all thy heart, and with all thy soul, and with all thy mind. This is the first and great commandment. And the second is like unto it. Thou shalt love thy neighbor as thyself. On these two commandments hang all the law and the prophets.

Luke 23: 34-KJV Then said Jesus, Father forgive them; for they know not what they do.

We will all be accountable for how we treat each other and how we take care of the gifts God has given us. In Matthew 18:6, 7KJV But whoso shall offend one of these little ones which believe in me, it were better for him that a millstone were hanged about his neck, and that he were drowned in the depth of the sea. Woe unto the world because of offences! For it must needs be that offenses come; but woe to that man by whom the offence cometh!

People have other issues in their lives which these courts don't consider. Frank and Alice were being harassed by a neighbor, who was an attorney, and was dragging them to court because he wanted property that he had no right to. So not only were they being harassed by the Child Support Courts but also were paying attorney fees for an attorney neighbor taking them to court unjustly. How can you have a job when you must take time out to go to court? Alice had a full-time job but worked a night shift, so she had to waste so many of her mornings going to court for one issue or another. This is why Frank couldn't stay in a day job, he was being pulled into court by his ex-wife (which occurred during the day) and a neighbor who had an address behind their house and wanted to use their driveway instead of what was given to him to use to get to his house. Child Support courts totally interfere with people lives and their ability to work and support their families. The men who walk out on their families and leave a woman the responsibility of raising the children they brought into the world together needs to be accountable for helping with the care of the children. Women who walk out on marriages should also be made accountable for helping with the children.

If this can be done better by separating the children and each parent taking responsibility or if in the case which the parents have addiction problems or abuse issues and need help. This is where family members should step in without having to go through the court system. These children are someone's grandchildren and if need be, the grandparents need to step up and help these children. I have heard of situations where the relatives who are willing to take care of the children have to go to court and then become foster parents in order to take care of members of their own families. Then the state pays the family members to take care of their own relatives plus the state gives free health insurance to the child. No wonder the states are overtaxing the working person. This is wrong. The children are a part of you going into the future. To be future leaders or people that can help make this a better world when raised in the right environment. Being loved and cared for will help them be better parents and better people.

The churches and each community used to take care of families in need. We need to go back to that. As a nation we all need to turn back to God and get on our knees and pray.

Dear Heavenly Father,

I am a sinner. I ask you to forgive me of my sins. I believe Jesus Christ shed his blood and died for my sin. I invite Jesus Christ to come into my heart and to be my personal Lord and Savior. Fill the emptiness in me with your Holy Spirit. Lord help me to trust you, love you, live my life for you, turn from my sin and to understand your grace, mercy and peace. Thank you, Lord. In Jesus name I pray. Amen

John 14: 6 KJV Jesus saith unto him, I am the way, the truth, and the life; no man cometh unto the Father, but by me.

WORKS CITED

C.S. Lovett. Unequally Yoked Wives. Copyrighted 1968

Meese, Edwin. The Heritage Guide to the Constitution. Washington: Regnery Publishing, 2005

Ritchie, Donald A., JusticeLearning.org. Our Constitution, New York: Oxford U Publishing, 2006

Definitions from online dictionaries

Scripture from King James Version Bible by Thomas Nelson Publishers Copyright 1984,1977

Divorce-Father's Rights by George Coppolo

American Heritage Dictionary

Child Support Arrearage Guide (effective August 1, 2005)

Printed in the United States
by Baker & Taylor Publisher Services

Printed in the United States
by Baker & Taylor Publisher Services